KETO LIKE A CHEF

SHOWSTOPPING RECIPES FOR YOUR KETO TABLE

JASON RAFFIN

Published by Flashpoint™ Books, Seattle
www.flashpointbooks.com

Produced by Girl Friday Productions

Design: Paul Barrett, Keith Schikore, Hans Bennewitz, and James Van Kriedt
Photographs: Keith Schikore
Production editorial: Abi Pollokoff
Project management: Emilie Sandoz-Voyer

Image credits: All photos by Keith Schikore except
page 162 by Tsar Nicoulai Caviar

ISBN (hardcover): 978-1-959411-56-7
ISBN (ebook): 978-1-959411-57-4

Library of Congress Control Number: 2024909488

First edition

To my friends, family, friends who are family,
the Maui community, and the people who
don't settle for the status quo

CONTENTS

Go Fast
Don't

INTRODUCTION

So, you decided to venture into the world of keto.

I know it can seem a bit intimidating, but don't worry. I'm here to tell you that not only is eating keto doable, it can also be both tasty and culinarily exciting. Through a process of sometimes wild experimentation and just having fun cooking within these guidelines, I developed dozens of amazing recipes to make eating keto a dining experience that could rival what you can find in any fancy restaurant.

This book is both a celebration of keto food at its finest and a documentation of the food I ate over a period of three months. I had such success losing a stubborn twenty pounds I'd been struggling with since high school that I knew I had to share the food I was making—and the style of cooking I was exploring.

I am a chef with more than a decade and a half of professional experience running restaurants and building food programs, and after searching through all the resources available for keto meals, I felt that they were missing a level of finesse and creativity. With keto, I stumbled upon a unique challenge, which morphed into the opportunity to share my style of using incredible sauces, restrained presentation, and farm-fresh ingredients to create unique dishes.

This book is dedicated to those searching to lose fat responsibly and also enjoy the process. When you're eating keto, you'll find that cooking for yourself is essential. Many restaurants hide carbohydrates in basic dishes, and these will kick you out of the ketosis game. It's important to love the food you eat, because it makes the journey to feeling your best that much more enjoyable. While making great food doesn't mean that you need to spend a ton of time perfecting the aesthetic of every morsel, it definitely doesn't hurt to add more attention to presentation, especially when serving others.

Over the course of writing this book, I had a helpful test subject in my photographer and best friend, Keith. Using mainly these recipes, he lost fifteen pounds of fat in two months. But Keith knew what he was getting into. You know a keto recipe is just right when the person eating it has no idea they are eating keto. These exciting dishes will keep even the most skeptical palates entertained enough to forget about the carbs. Big flavors satiate big appetites, and these recipes helped me achieve my goals of obtaining the body I never dreamed possible without sacrificing flavor and joy in the kitchen. I gained energy and began establishing a new relationship with my body. The key is to make it fun and delicious.

Every dish in these pages was created with a totally freestyle approach and then captured with the camera. Our goal was always to make beautiful food that was delicious and fun to eat, so don't get the impression that we made this book with our pinkies out. Sure, the majority of your keto meals might be composed of easy keto wins like bacon-and-cheese omelets, burgers on keto bread, and salads. This book offers a creative outlet for those who love to cook and want to eat like they would at a five-star restaurant while still losing weight.

I've included macronutrients for a single serving of each recipe, but note that not all the ratios of the macronutrients add up to exactly what is needed to sustain ketosis. Take care to adjust the rest of your diet to make sure the numbers work for you. Get inspired, get excited to eat, and enjoy the weight loss process. We did.

WHO AM I?

My name is Jason, and I am a keto convert. The keto diet allowed me to feel I had control over my weight for the first time in my life. I have been husky since middle school, and I just assumed it was genetic. I have always been obsessed with food.

My first professional restaurant experience was spending a day cooking at Yank Sing, a famous San Francisco dim sum restaurant, at the age of eleven. After putting on my first chef coat and spending time in the basement with all the grannies folding dumplings, my future in restaurants was destined. I spent high school cooking at various Bay Area establishments, then went on to college at the University of Massachusetts Amherst. There, I majored in restaurant management while working in the university's kitchens to pay my bills. Next, I attended the Culinary Institute of America at Greystone in Saint Helena, California.

After cutting my teeth working in kitchens in Napa Valley and San Francisco, I decided to open my own restaurant. As a part owner of Scotland Yard at the age of twenty-four, I was featured in Zagat's "30 Under 30" and went on to build various culinary programs across San Francisco. After many successful openings, I decided to travel the world and build my skills and scope.

My travels started in January 2020, when I had planned to begin a two-year trek across Europe starting in Italy. But first I would spend a little time in

Hawaii. Unfortunately, a worldwide pandemic had other plans for me.

Constructing a cookbook was never the plan when I arrived in Hawaii that January. Moving to Hawaii was never the plan, either. When COVID-19 hit, I was forced to stay put and rethink my larger travel plans. Stuck with only Keith for company, I decided to experiment with keto.

I had always been active, but historically I had enjoyed cooking with no restraint regarding calories to get the most delicious results. I eventually began focusing my energy toward crafting a healthier lifestyle, and while exercise and a balanced diet felt great, they never gave me the results I wanted. I would strength train regularly and vigorously but never could drop to a healthy BMI.

The process was very demoralizing. After years of following all the rules, I talked to an occupational therapist friend of mine and learned about the very real results that could be attained by following a ketogenic diet. I had always scoffed at what I considered to be a "fad diet." But my interest was piqued by her reverence, and it provoked me to consider experimenting. I planned to only partly stick to the diet, but my friend warned against this approach vigorously. You either follow the diet or you don't do it at all, she told me. The intensity of her caution made an impact on me.

What really convinced me to take the leap was the counsel of my old chef, who had taken an interest in my naivete on the issue. He explained how, by adhering to a keto lifestyle, he had lost 130 pounds since the last time I'd seen him. (He is six feet six and used to resemble a handsome Andre the Giant.) I listened to doctors, of course, but I followed my chef. That day I truly began my research. At first I was flabbergasted at how many carbs there are in such a diverse array of foods. Once I knew which ingredients had the least carbs, I began to plan menus in my head. As a chef, I enjoy parameters because they force me to come up with innovative solutions. I went to the local market and was surprised to see a section dedicated to low-carb foods in rural Maui. I stocked up and began to create. I cooked using the terroir, local farms, industry connections, and whatever was available in close proximity and quickly discovered how rewarding keto could be as a means to lose weight and enjoy creative cooking.

The first month, I lost eight pounds and 2.5 percent body fat. I was stunned. I had no idea how much fat was hidden around my body. My legs got to a point where I could see muscle definition. This revelation and success were potent, and the food I was cooking was out-of-this-world delicious. I wanted to show others how to navigate the keto lifestyle through the lens of a chef—and create a resource for those who want to challenge themselves to make amazing low-carb food.

SOBRIETY

The lifestyle of a chef takes a toll on the mind and spirit. High-stress environments breed unhealthy

consequences, and learning to cope with these afflictions was an awakening moment in my career.

Drinking was never a huge problem for me, but I overindulged frequently. I would show up to work early, work my ass off for fourteen hours or more, and then head toward light debauchery. This lifestyle is built for those who enjoy the fringe of society, which is where I've always felt most comfortable. I enjoyed the solace of a controlled chaos and then replicated the adrenaline rush endured in the kitchen with post-shift drinks.

The culinary world closes you off to holidays, family, weekends, and normal society, so if you like any of those things, do not enter the professional kitchen. I, for one, adore missing functions, birthdays, and the weekend hullabaloo. Most of my cohorts were the same way. The decision to change my late-night drinking hit me when I moved to Hawaii and away from distractions, direct connections to trouble, and the all-night parties I was so accustomed to.

After touching down in paradise, I immediately recognized this as an opportunity to explore life from a sober perspective. I did not have my first drink in Hawaii until I had lived there for thirteen months. I had no idea of the incredible transformation I would make over the next year, exploring emotions, inner peace, unwavering inspiration, and flow-state creation. I lost a couple of friends during this process, as they were appealing only through the lens of drunken activities, but I also made life-changing friends who joined in my sober endeavors. Instead of abusing my body and brain, I nurtured myself, focused on love and compassion, and gave my body what it needed. If it weren't for sobriety, I would not be writing this book today.

So how does this relate to keto? Most alcoholic drinks have a lot of carbohydrates, the exception being a few no-carb brands. Ditching the booze tends to be half the battle for most people working on a diet or their general health. Want to lose five pounds of fat in a month? Lose the booze.

COOKING FOR OUR MAUI COMMUNITY

After it was clear that Hawaii would be my home for the foreseeable future, I redirected my professional culinary efforts. I wanted to invest in the loving community of Maui, which was hit particularly hard by the drop in tourism during the COVID-19 pandemic, and I started envisioning ways to help the community to nurture itself. With this in mind, I founded the Chef Collective for Covid in June 2020.

During the months we were active, we raised more than $25,000 to help support local farms. The Chef Collective gave local furloughed chefs the opportunity to create guest chef dinners that would be delivered to vulnerable members of our community free of charge. We partnered with the local food bank affiliate, Lahaina Baptist Church, which had the infrastructure in place to be able to identify the most vulnerable members of the community. They also had the resources available for organizing groups of volunteers to deliver the food directly to the doorsteps of hungry people.

The Chef Collective gave generations of chefs from different restaurants the opportunity to give back to the community. All the food was hand-harvested from various local farms, and we educated all the chefs, sous chefs, and cooks on sustainable organic farming practices and offered the experience of doing true farm-to-table cooking. With the determination and support of new lifelong friends, we were able to deliver refined, multicourse tasting menus to thousands of Maui residents for free during a time of uncertainty and despair.

Then, in 2023, when we finally felt like our feet were back under us, we got hit harder than ever.

On August 8, 2023, as I was engrossed in producing this book, things took a sudden and devastating turn. My home and business were among many others lost in the inferno that swept through Lahaina. My girlfriend and I narrowly escaped as wildfires encroached upon our neighborhood, forcing us to flee in the chaos. We were fortunate to encounter a Good Samaritan who, with his car, moved a massive boulder that had been blocking a dirt bike path above the city limits, allowing our escape. Along with a caravan of survivors, we navigated through hazardous conditions, including downed power lines from a concurrent hurricane. As night fell and the flames illuminated the sky, I realized it would be the last time I saw Lahaina intact. I had salvaged only a few possessions, including my knives and passport.

Determined to assist those in need, I arranged for my girlfriend's departure from Maui, knowing my place was here, amid the devastation. Stripped of my catering equipment, and with cherished establishments reduced to rubble, I found solace in the unwavering support of allies like Hua Momona Farms.

In collaboration with the farm's owner, Gary Grube, we mobilized swiftly, transforming fresh produce into nourishment for displaced residents. Within hours, Gary's newly outfitted kitchen became a beacon of hope, churning out hundreds of meals daily. Fueled by the collective spirit of volunteers and guided by a vision of long-term recovery, we forged partnerships and implemented sustainable initiatives to address the enduring needs of our community.

Operating around the clock, seven days a week, we rallied hundreds of volunteers, producing up to 750 meals every other day. As the magnitude of the crisis settled in, we transitioned to a sustainable model, partnering with organizations like Hungry Heroes Hawaii and welcoming tourist assistance at the farm.

Our program evolved to encompass farming, kitchen work, and meal delivery. Within six months of the tragedy, we had prepared and delivered forty thousand meals. Grateful for the opportunity to contribute, I now serve as executive chef of the Hua Momona Foundation, spearheading their food security efforts in Maui.

HOW TO KETO

When I first read all the rules of keto, I was very skeptical, which is my nature. I've always believed in moderation and diversity in cooking. Cutting out nearly entire food groups and grains to eat more fats is counterintuitive and intimidating—but the science is indisputable.

Ketosis happens when the body gets its energy by burning fat—not glucose, which is what it normally defaults to. In order for the human body to enter ketosis, you must eat 75 percent of your calories from fat, 20 percent from protein, and only the remaining 5 percent from carbohydrates. There are apps available to help you calculate your maximum daily caloric intake, and the key is to stay right around those ratios. When you exercise while eating keto, you are burning fat directly. I recommend getting a smartwatch to monitor your daily exercise, making small goals that you can accomplish every day. For example, I try to walk a minimum of ten thousand steps daily.

One of the most important elements to help you safely and pleasantly enter ketosis is to drink tons of water. Being dehydrated and lacking electrolytes can cause flu-like symptoms. I bring my water flask with me everywhere I go.

To be able to easily track the macronutrients you're consuming, I recommend getting a macro calculator app on your phone as well. It is important to record and calculate anything you are putting into your body. Utilizing keto strips to monitor the keto levels in your body also helps to determine whether or not you're on track. I also like to use a scale to track weekly goals and body fat percentage. The main point is to keep consistent data. This all may sound like a lot, but trust me: follow the rules and you will see big results!

Be warned: following a keto diet can be expensive! Granted, I indulge in a variety of diverse products. But proteins and high-fat foods are generally more expensive than carbohydrate-rich foods. There's a reason why entire aisles at the store, generally in the center, are completely carb driven. Be prepared to have more expensive groceries. File it under investing in yourself. That being said, not every meal needs to be a knockout in terms of luxe ingredients and garnishes. This book is meant to inspire, and though I ate these dishes over the course of three months, I also made quick, easy meals. No one has the time or energy to make elaborate dishes every single day for breakfast, lunch, and dinner. Most days I ate a simple breakfast with MCT oil–infused coffee.

My keto journey was certainly not flawless, and I screwed up a couple of times by not following the rules stated above, especially in not tallying my macros. In restaurants, chefs know that a mistake is not a problem; it is how you recover from it that matters. Not following the rules will knock off days of progress. It's a bummer, but it happens. Forgive yourself, move forward, and be vigilant.

KEY INGREDIENTS

ANIMAL FATS

Duck, pork, chicken, bacon, pan drippings

As I roast meats to cook for friends, I always use a rack and collect the cooking liquids underneath. That's an extra-credit flavor right there. Don't throw it away!

CRUCIFEROUS VEGETABLES

Broccoli, cauliflower, bok choy, brussels sprouts

I like to eat lots of vegetables because they are low in calories and high in fiber. It is important to get fiber through this process. Just be careful, as there are hidden carbohydrates in these foods.

ANIMAL SKINS

Salmon, chicken, pork rinds, puffed beef tendon

One of the areas of keto that can be difficult is lacking the crunch from flours or grains. These crispy skins give that potato chip feel with none of the guilt. It's important to treat yourself to a nice crunch!

KETO BREADS

Sliced bread, buns, pancakes

I love sandwiches, burgers, and Benedicts. Without a bread substitute, none of these can be accomplished sufficiently. Some brands put out some amazing products; others are inedible. These are my favorite brands: Sola, Oroweat, and Keto Culture.

PROTEINS

Poultry, beef, tofu, pork, lamb, eggs, fish, cheese, peanuts

PICKLED VEGETABLES

Sauerkraut, garlic pickles, kimchi
Having tart, low-calorie accoutrements is a very nice way to balance all the fat that this diet requires.

SUGAR SUBSTITUTES

Swerve, stevia, allulose, monk fruit, erythritol
I don't consider myself as having a sweet tooth, but after a while you miss the taste of sweetness. These artificial sweeteners, when used intelligently and with purpose, help add that sugary kick and satiate those desires.

ALTERNATIVE FLOURS

Almond, coconut, psyllium husk, lupin, flaxseed meal

BREAKFAST

LOBSTER BENEDICT WITH FENNEL BÉARNAISE

When I go out to eat breakfast or brunch, it is hard for me not to order a Benedict. So much is revealed about a restaurant by the quality of their hollandaise, the texture of the egg, and the overall composition of the Benedict. Be sure to take your time in the construction of this recipe, as the presentation really sells the dish. I like to add a bit of old-school funk to the dish by upgrading the classic hollandaise to a modern béarnaise, and I personally believe that the egg should be fully covered in sauce. Tarragon is typically the determining factor for a béarnaise, but here I opted to use fennel, which is in the same anise flavor family.

SERVES 2

MACROS PER SERVING

Net carbs: 11 grams
Protein: 42 grams
Fat: 51 grams
Calories: 671

BLISTERED KALE

- 1 bunch kale, stems removed and leaves roughly torn
- 2 tablespoons chopped garlic
- 2 tablespoons olive oil
- 1 tablespoon sambal
- 1 tablespoon fish sauce
- 1 teaspoon lemon zest
- 1 teaspoon salt

KETO BISCUITS

- 1 cup (96 grams) almond flour, chilled
- 2 tablespoons oat fiber
- 1½ teaspoons baking powder
- 1 teaspoon salt
- 2 tablespoons unsalted butter, frozen
- ¾ cup (177 milliliters) egg whites, chilled and lightly beaten
- 1 egg yolk, beaten
- 1 tablespoon unsalted butter, melted

FENNEL BÉARNAISE

- 1 shallot, chopped
- ½ bulb fennel, chopped
- 1 cup (237 milliliters) keto wine
- 1 tablespoon fennel seed
- 1 tablespoon white wine vinegar
- 1 teaspoon black peppercorns
- 2 tablespoons water
- 4 egg yolks, beaten
- ¾ cup (172 grams) unsalted butter, melted and clarified
- 1 teaspoon hot sauce
- Salt
- Squeeze of lemon juice

TO ASSEMBLE

- Oil, for frying (such as canola)
- 1 cup (89 grams) finely julienned leeks
- 2 keto biscuits
- Unsalted butter for sautéing
- ½ pound (227 grams) cooked lobster meat
- 2 tablespoons white vinegar
- 4 eggs
- 1 cup (135 grams) blistered kale
- ½ cup (118 milliliters) fennel béarnaise
- Fennel fronds, for garnish

BLISTERED KALE

Bring a large pot of lightly salted water to a boil. Blanch the kale in the boiling water for 1 minute and then remove to an ice bath for 2 minutes. Wring the kale out by hand and put into a large bowl. Add the remaining ingredients and let marinate for at least 1 hour, or up to 3 days. If you have a grill, grill the kale over high heat for about 1 minute until blackened and set aside. Alternatively, sauté over high heat in a dry cast-iron pan for 1 minute, or until blistered, and set aside.

KETO BISCUITS

Preheat the oven to 400°F (204°C). Cut the butter into pea-sized pieces and keep cold. In a medium bowl, mix the almond flour, oat fiber, baking powder, and salt. Add the butter and use your pointer finger and thumb to squish the butter pieces and flour mixture together to make flat disks about the size of half a dime (0.35″ [9 mm] in diameter). Add the egg whites and mix until it just comes together. Spoon into ring molds, brush with the egg yolk, and bake for 15 minutes, or until golden brown. Take the biscuits out of the oven and remove the ring molds. Immediately brush with the melted butter and move to a rack to cool.

FENNEL BÉARNAISE

In a small saucepan over medium heat, combine the shallot, fennel, wine, fennel seed, vinegar, and peppercorns and reduce until *au sec* (almost dry). Add the water, strain the mixture into a medium metal bowl and discard the solids, and allow the liquid to cool slightly. Add the egg yolks to the liquid and transfer to a double boiler. Once the water is simmering, whisk the egg yolk mixture constantly over the heat for 10 seconds, then off for 10 seconds; continue in this way for 10 minutes, or until the mixture has doubled in size and turned pale. Slowly whisk in the clarified butter 1 tablespoon at a time, continuing to remove from the heat every 10 seconds to avoid overcooking the egg mixture. Make sure each tablespoon of butter is fully incorporated before adding the next. Season with hot sauce, salt, and lemon juice. Set aside.

TO ASSEMBLE

Add about 2″ (5 cm) of oil and the leeks to a large cast-iron pan, then place over medium-low heat and slowly bring the oil up to 300°F (149°C) over 15 minutes, stirring occasionally to maintain even cooking and prevent sticking. Cook until golden brown and bubbles stop forming, then remove to a paper-towel-lined plate to cool. Split the keto biscuits in half and, in a large cast-iron pan, sauté in the butter over medium heat until golden brown on each side. Set the biscuits aside, add the lobster to the pan, and warm for 1 minute. Remove the lobster and allow the pan to cool. Add the vinegar to a large pot of water and heat to just below a boil. Poach the eggs in the acidulated water for 3½ minutes and remove from the water. Stack each half of the biscuits with the lobster, kale, and eggs, and then top each egg with a spoonful of the fennel béarnaise. Finish with a garnish of the crispy leeks and fennel fronds.

SERVES 2

MACROS PER SERVING

Net carbs: 10 grams
Protein: 35 grams
Fat: 55 grams
Calories: 675

SPICY PULLED PORK BENEDICT

Here is another variation on one of my breakfast favorites. This time I went with a more aggressive style that highlights one of my go-to keto meats: pulled pork. You can make your own fermented chilies with some seasonal farmers' market peppers and use that or another fermented-chili paste in place of the sambal here. Crisping up the pork is key, and it's best when it isn't over-braised. The hollandaise sauce is heat- and time-sensitive and should be done as close as possible to the time of serving the dish.

PULLED PORK

- 1 tablespoon black peppercorns
- 1 tablespoon fennel seed
- 1 tablespoon mustard seed
- 2 tablespoons onion powder
- 1 tablespoon paprika
- 1 tablespoon garlic powder
- 4 tablespoons Swerve brown sugar
- 2 tablespoons salt
- 1 tablespoon chicken bouillon powder
- 2 pounds (907 grams) pork butt
- 2 tablespoons bacon fat or butter

GOCHUJANG OIL

- 4 tablespoons Korean chili flakes (such as Wang brand)
- ¼ cup (59 milliliters) canola oil

FRESNO CHILI CURLS

- 2 Fresno chilies

FERMENTED-CHILI HOLLANDAISE

- 1 shallot, minced
- 1 cup (237 milliliters) keto wine
- 2 tablespoons white wine vinegar
- 1 teaspoon black peppercorns
- 2 tablespoons water
- 3 egg yolks
- ¾ cup (172 grams) unsalted butter, melted and clarified
- 3 tablespoons sambal (such as Huy Fong sambal oelek)
- 2 tablespoons sriracha
- 1 tablespoon hot sauce (such as Tabasco)
- Salt
- Squeeze of lemon juice

TO ASSEMBLE

- 2 keto biscuits (page 22)
- Unsalted butter for sautéing
- 1 cup (240 grams) pulled pork
- 2 tablespoons white vinegar
- 4 eggs
- 6 tablespoons fermented-chili hollandaise
- 4 teaspoons Fresno chili curls
- Purple micro basil, for garnish
- 2 tablespoons gochujang oil

PULLED PORK

Preheat the oven to 350°F (177°C). Dry toast the peppercorns, fennel, and mustard seed in a small skillet over medium heat until fragrant. Grind and then mix with the remaining spices and the brown sugar, salt, and chicken bouillon. Smother the pork butt in bacon fat or butter and coat heavily in the spice mixture, rubbing it in on all sides. Place into a roasting pan and roast uncovered for 1½ hours. Remove from the oven, reduce temperature to 275°F (135°C), cover the entire pan in foil, and roast for another 3 hours, or until meat is caramelized brown and easily shreddable and the internal temperature reaches 205°F (96°C). Set aside to cool. Once cooled, shred the pork and transfer to a covered container in the fridge until ready to serve.

GOCHUJANG OIL

While the pork is cooking, mix the chili flakes and oil in a small pot and heat on low until the oil simmers. Cool the mixture to room temperature and strain with a fine-mesh strainer. Set aside.

FRESNO CHILI CURLS

Deseed the peppers by cutting them into flat strips and cutting out the membrane. Slice thinly—as small as possible—on the bias and then add to a large bowl of ice water. Let chill in the fridge for at least an hour.

FERMENTED-CHILI HOLLANDAISE

In a small saucepan over medium heat, combine the shallot, keto wine, vinegar, and peppercorns and reduce until *au sec* (almost dry). Add the water, strain the mixture into a large metal bowl and discard the solids, and allow the liquid to cool slightly. Add the egg yolks to the liquid and transfer to a double boiler. Once the water is simmering, whisk the egg yolk mixture constantly over the heat for 10 seconds, then off for 10 seconds; continue in this way for 10 minutes, or until the mixture has doubled in size and turned pale. Slowly whisk in the clarified butter 1 tablespoon at a time, continuing to remove from the heat every 10 seconds to avoid overcooking the egg mixture. Make sure each tablespoon of butter is fully incorporated before adding the next. Season with sambal, sriracha, hot sauce, salt, and lemon juice. Set aside.

TO ASSEMBLE

Split the keto biscuits in half and, in a large cast-iron pan, sauté in butter over medium heat until golden brown on each side. Set the biscuits aside, raise the heat to medium-high, and sear the pork on all sides until crispy, about 4 minutes. Add the vinegar to a large pot of water and heat to just below a boil. Poach the eggs in the acidulated water for 3½ minutes and remove from the water. Add the pulled pork to the biscuit halves and top with the poached eggs, fermented-chili hollandaise, Fresno chili curls, and micro basil, then drizzle with the gochujang oil.

CHEESE SOUFFLÉ

2 tablespoons unsalted butter, divided
2 tablespoons almond flour, divided
4 egg yolks, lightly beaten
½ cup (118 milliliters) heavy cream
¼ cup (59 milliliters) whole milk
2 tablespoons Brie cheese, rind removed
2 egg whites
¼ teaspoon cream of tartar
1 tablespoon Tsar Nicoulai Estate Caviar

Soufflés represent the peak of French cooking snobbery. They are fickle, time-sensitive, precise, and demand the full attention of those serving and eating them to be enjoyed fully. I love them. This rendition is very basic and can be adjusted in so many ways to fit ideal flavor combinations. I kept it simple and luxurious with Brie and a quenelle (an elegant spoonful) of estate caviar. It's never too early to indulge in some Tsar Nicoulai.

SERVES 3

MACROS PER SERVING

Net carbs: 5 grams
Protein: 12 grams
Fat: 35 grams
Calories: 383

Preheat the oven to 375°F (191°C). Use about 1 teaspoon of the butter to coat the inside of three 6-ounce (170-milliliter) ramekins and sprinkle in almond flour to coat (about ½ teaspoon per ramekin), shaking out the excess. Place the egg yolks in a small bowl. In a medium saucepan over medium-low heat, cook the remaining butter and almond flour for 1 minute and then whisk in the cream, milk, and Brie. Once fully emulsified, remove from the heat and add ¼ cup (59 milliliters) of the mixture to the egg yolks and mix; it should not curdle. Once fully blended, add the yolk mixture back into the pan over medium-low heat and whisk until fully combined. Remove from the heat and cool to room temperature. In a large bowl, beat the egg whites with the cream of tartar until stiff peaks form. Working in batches, add the beaten egg whites one-third at a time to the cooled Brie mixture and fold to fully incorporate. Spoon the batter into the prepared ramekins, filling three-fourths of the way up. Bake for 20 minutes, or until golden brown. Serve immediately, topped with a spoonful of Tsar Nicoulai Estate Caviar.

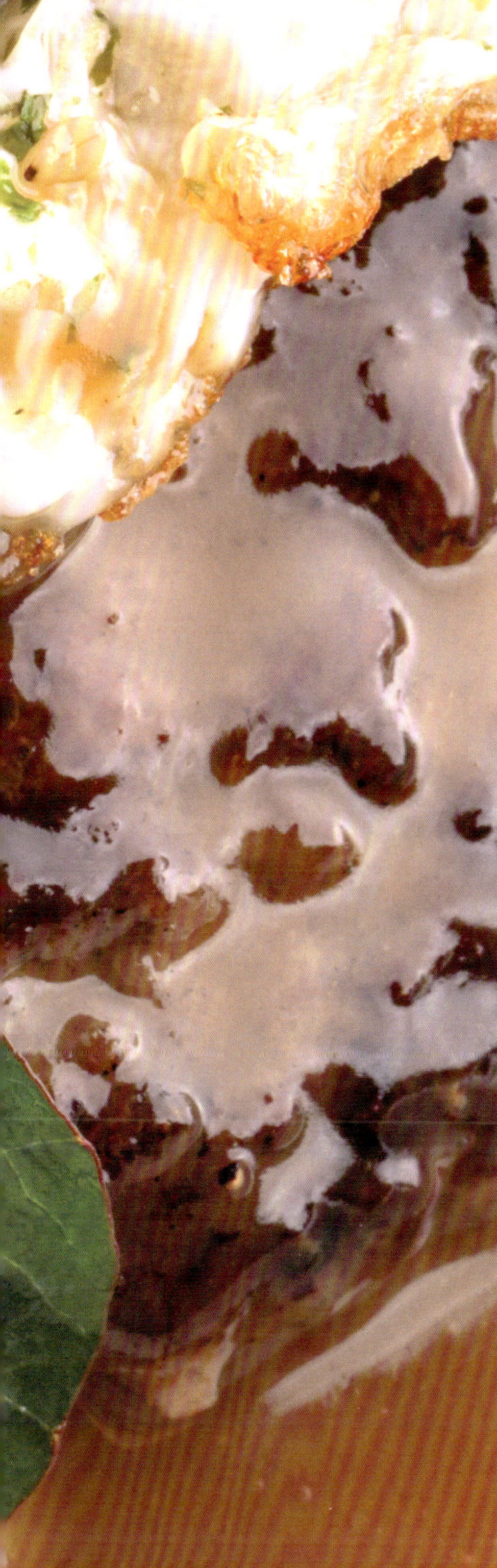

SERVES 2

MACROS PER SERVING

Net carbs: 8 grams
Protein: 41 grams
Fat: 48 grams
Calories: 628

LOCO MOCO

As a current resident of Hawaii, I feel obligated to add a loco moco recipe that would satisfy my cravings. Cauliflower rice works well as a vehicle for all the flavor in this classic dish. What really ties this dish together, however, is the beef jus, which can be used on just about any dish to add an unctuous layer of flavor. For the beef patties and eggs, use a cast-iron pan to allow for deep browning. Color equals flavor, and flavor keeps you satisfied.

BEEF JUS

4 ounces (113 grams) 80/20 ground beef
1 cup (237 milliliters) keto white wine or Shaoxing wine
3 quarts (2.8 liters) beef stock
2 tablespoons Dijon mustard
2 tablespoons heavy cream
1 tablespoon fish sauce
1 tablespoon fennel seed
1 tablespoon coriander seed
1 tablespoon chopped garlic
½ bunch thyme

TO ASSEMBLE

4 cups (428 grams) chopped cauliflower
3 tablespoons olive oil, divided
2 (4-ounce [113-gram]) beef patties, 80 percent lean
2 eggs
2 teaspoons furikake, divided
½ cup (118 milliliters) beef jus
Microgreens, for garnish

BEEF JUS

In a large pot over medium-high heat, sear the beef on all sides until browned, about 3 minutes, then chop up the meat in the pot with a spatula and deglaze with the wine. Add the remaining ingredients and reduce over medium heat for about an hour until it is about 2 cups (473 milliliters). Strain with a chinois or fine-mesh strainer and reserve.

TO ASSEMBLE

In a food processor, pulse the cauliflower until the consistency of rice. Cook the cauliflower with 2 tablespoons of the olive oil in a large nonstick pan for 3 to 5 minutes until softened but not mushy. Set aside. Heat a large cast-iron pan until very hot. Add the beef patties and smash them with the back of a metal spatula. Cook undisturbed until browned on the bottom and almost fully cooked, 4 to 6 minutes. Scrape the patties off the bottom of the pan with a metal spatula, making sure to keep the bottom intact. Flip the patties and cook until desired doneness, 3 to 4 minutes for medium-rare. Clean the pan and get it scorching hot again. Add the remaining 1 tablespoon oil, crack the eggs into the pan, and liberally season with about 1 teaspoon furikake. Remove once cooked to desired doneness. Pile riced cauliflower on the bottom of 2 plates and top each with a patty, an egg, the remaining furikake, and beef jus. Garnish with the microgreens.

SERVES 1 TO 2

MACROS PER SERVING

Net carbs: 12 grams
Protein: 20 grams
Fat: 40 grams
Calories: 488

SAFFRON CRAB OMELET WITH TOFU HOME-FRY

Omelets are a no-brainer for breakfast. With the addition of crab, avocado, and a saffron cream, this omelet is sure to point your day in the right direction. I opted for Dungeness crab for this rendition, but feel free to cook whatever crab is available. There are many varieties that come from a can that are delicious and won't cause you to take a second mortgage on your house. Real saffron may not be readily available, so feel free to experiment with the sauce as well. It's very basic and lends itself to many varieties. For instance, as an alternative, I recommend sautéing some spicy red Thai curry paste in oil before adding the cream.

HOME-FRY SPICE

1 tablespoon white peppercorns
1 tablespoon coriander seed
1 tablespoon mustard seed
1 tablespoon fennel seed
2 tablespoons salt
1 tablespoon chili flakes
1 tablespoon garlic powder
1 tablespoon onion powder
1 tablespoon hot paprika

SAFFRON CREAM

½ cup (118 milliliters) heavy cream
1 teaspoon lemon zest
1 teaspoon lemon juice
¼ teaspoon saffron threads
Salt and pepper

TOFU HOME-FRY

1 cup (124 grams) diced zucchini
1 cup (170 grams) diced bell peppers
2 tablespoons olive oil
3 tablespoons home-fry spice, divided
1 cup (252 grams) diced extra-firm tofu (small dice)
1 quart (946 milliliters) oil, for frying (such as canola, bran, or peanut oil)
10 sage leaves

TO ASSEMBLE

¼ cup (36 grams) pulled Dungeness crab meat
1 teaspoon fish sauce
1 teaspoon lemon zest
1 teaspoon lemon juice
Large pinch of salt
3 eggs
1 tablespoon unsalted butter
½ avocado, sliced
¼ cup (59 milliliters) saffron cream
2 teaspoons chopped fresh dill
½ cup (124 grams) tofu home-fry

HOME-FRY SPICE

In a small skillet over medium heat, toast the peppercorns, coriander, mustard, and fennel until fragrant. Grind and mix with the salt, chili flakes, garlic powder, onion powder, and paprika until well blended.

SAFFRON CREAM

In a small saucepan over medium-low heat, whisk together the cream, lemon zest, lemon juice, saffron, salt, and pepper and cook, stirring frequently, until reduced by half. Set aside.

TOFU HOME-FRY

Preheat the oven to 400°F (204°C). Place a baking sheet in the oven and allow it to get scorching hot. In a medium bowl, toss the zucchini and peppers with the olive oil and 2 tablespoons of the home-fry spice. Remove the scorching-hot sheet from the oven and add the vegetables. There should be audible sizzling. Return to the oven and cook for 10 minutes, or until the vegetables are browned, then remove the vegetables from the sheet. Add the raw tofu and oil to a large nonstick pan and place over medium heat. Cook for 10 to 15 minutes, stirring occasionally to prevent sticking, until the tofu has lost much of its moisture and reduced by half in size. Once fully browned, remove the tofu from the oil, reserve the oil, and immediately toss the tofu with the remaining tablespoon of spice. Taste and adjust seasoning according to preference. Fry the sage leaves in the remaining oil in the pan at 325°F (163°C) until lightly browned, remove from the oil, and then toss them with the other ingredients. Set aside.

TO ASSEMBLE

In a small bowl, mix the crab with the fish sauce, lemon zest, lemon juice, and salt. In another medium bowl, whisk the eggs until fully combined. Warm a large nonstick pan over medium-high heat and add the butter. Once melted (but not brown), add the eggs and cook, continually scraping the sides with a spatula and pulling the firm eggs to the center to allow the raw eggs to run and cook underneath. When there is no longer any runny raw egg visible, season the omelet with salt and flip quickly, then immediately remove from the pan. Add the avocado and crab to the center and then fold the eggs over the top into a half circle. Top with the saffron cream and garnish with the dill. Serve alongside the warm tofu home-fry.

SERVES 3

MACROS PER SERVING

Net carbs: 8 grams
Protein: 24 grams
Fat: 40 grams
Calories: 486

EGG QUICHES

Quiches are great for feeding groups and can last in the fridge for multiple days as an easy snacking option. A good pie crust will make or break this recipe, and this one delivers. Make sure to parbake the crust until it is thoroughly browned before adding the eggs. If bacon isn't your thing, then we probably won't get along, but you can try adding some roasted mushrooms or crisped seitan to add that needed savory bite.

KETO PIE CRUST

Coconut oil spray or butter for greasing
1 cup (96 grams) almond flour
1 cup (112 grams) shredded Parmesan
1 egg
½ teaspoon baking soda
Pinch of salt
¼ cup (57 grams) unsalted butter, frozen

TO ASSEMBLE

1½ zucchini
3 individual cooked pie crusts
Heaping ½ cup (63 grams) crumbled cooked bacon
6 tablespoons shredded cheddar cheese
6 eggs
6 tablespoons whole milk
6 tablespoons heavy cream
1 sprig each oregano and thyme, plus more for garnish
Generous pinches of salt and pepper

KETO PIE CRUST

Grease three 4″ (10 cm) glass pie plates with either coconut oil spray or butter. Mix the almond flour, Parmesan, egg, baking soda, and salt together in a medium bowl. Grate the frozen butter and then fold it into the mixture. Cover the dough with plastic wrap and place in the freezer for 20 minutes. Preheat the oven to 350°F (177°C). Divide the dough into 3 pieces. On a surface dusted with almond flour or between 2 sheets of plastic wrap, roll out each piece of crust to about ¼″ (0.5 cm) thickness. Press into the prepared pie plates and poke all over with a fork. Bake for 15 minutes, or until golden brown. Remove from the oven and let cool slightly.

TO ASSEMBLE

Slice the zucchini thinly on a mandoline or with a vegetable slicer and roll into 3 circles. Place one zucchini circle in the center of each of the cooled pie crusts and sprinkle evenly with the bacon and cheese. In a large bowl, mix the eggs, milk, cream, oregano, thyme, salt, and pepper with a whisk. Pour the egg mixture into the pie crusts and bake at 350°F (177°C) for 45 minutes, or until golden brown. Let rest for at least 30 minutes at room temperature before serving. Season with additional salt and pepper and garnish with thyme and oregano.

STRAWBERRY PANCAKES

Pancakes, strawberries, and whipped butter . . . need I say more? This is one of those dishes that you enjoy so much it makes you marvel at the wizardry that is keto. I grew up near Watsonville, California, which is the strawberry hub of the United States. Finding top-quality strawberries for this recipe is half the battle. The other half is not eating five servings of this dish.

SERVES 2 TO 3

MACROS PER SERVING

Net carbs: 8 grams
Protein: 9 grams
Fat: 37 grams
Calories: 401

STRAWBERRY SYRUP

4 tablespoons sugar-free strawberry jam
5 strawberries, diced
1 tablespoon Swerve brown sugar
Pinch of salt

WHIPPED BUTTER

¼ cup (57 grams) unsalted butter at room temperature
2 tablespoons whole milk
3 tablespoons Swerve confectioners' sugar
Pinch of salt

PANCAKES

3 eggs
1 teaspoon cream of tartar
1 cup (96 grams) almond flour
¼ cup (60 grams) cream cheese
2 tablespoons Swerve brown sugar
2 teaspoons baking powder
1 teaspoon vanilla extract

TO ASSEMBLE

6 pancakes
¾ cup (108 grams) whipped butter
¾ cup (177 milliliters) strawberry syrup

STRAWBERRY SYRUP

Heat all the ingredients together in a small pan over medium heat for 5 minutes, stirring occasionally, until the strawberries have broken down and the syrup has thickened slightly. Remove from the heat and set aside.

WHIPPED BUTTER

Whisk the softened butter until it is fluffy and increases in volume. Add the milk and whisk until it is fully incorporated. Add the confectioners' sugar and salt and whisk to combine. Keep at room temperature.

PANCAKES

Separate the eggs and in a medium bowl mix the whites with the cream of tartar. With an electric mixer, beat until stiff peaks form and set aside. In a large bowl, mix the egg yolks with the remaining ingredients until well blended. Working in batches, fold in one-third of the beaten egg whites at a time until fully incorporated. Heat a medium pan over medium heat and coat with nonstick spray. Cook the pancake batter a few spoonfuls at a time to make silver-dollar-sized (1.5″ [38 mm] in diameter) pancakes, about 1 to 2 minutes per side, flipping when bubbles form on top. Coat the pan with cooking spray between batches.

TO ASSEMBLE

Place 2 or 3 pancakes on each plate with whipped butter and strawberry syrup on top.

COLA BBQ RIBS

This method of preparing ribs allows the best qualities of the meat to shine. The braising process breaks down the connective tissue, tenderizing the meat so well that it can be cut with a spoon. The frying creates a crunchy exterior, while the sticky sauce gives just enough sweetness and tang to offset the richness of the meat. This is a very nontraditional way of preparing ribs and the effort is worth it.

SERVES 3

MACROS PER SERVING

Net carbs: 6 grams
Protein: 45 grams
Fat: 23 grams
Calories: 411

RIB DRY RUB

- 2 tablespoons mustard seed
- 2 tablespoons black peppercorns
- 2 tablespoons coriander seed
- 4 tablespoons smoked paprika
- 4 tablespoons salt
- 2 tablespoons chili powder
- 2 tablespoons sweet paprika
- 2 tablespoons onion powder
- 1 tablespoon garlic powder
- ¾ tablespoon ground cumin

COLA RIB GLAZE

- 1 tablespoon black peppercorns
- 1 tablespoon coriander seed
- 1 (12-ounce [355-milliliter]) can of diet cola
- 3 cloves garlic
- 3 tablespoons fish sauce
- 1½ tablespoons soy sauce
- 1 tablespoon sriracha
- 1 tablespoon sherry vinegar

TO FINISH

- 1 rack baby back ribs
- 4 tablespoons rib dry rub
- 1 quart (946 milliliters) chicken stock
- Oil, for frying (such as canola, bran, or peanut)
- ½ cup (118 milliliters) cola rib glaze
- 3 tablespoons chopped roasted peanuts
- Micro mizuna, for garnish
- Lemon zest, for garnish

RIB DRY RUB

In a small skillet over medium heat, toast the mustard seed, peppercorns, and coriander seed until fragrant. Grind, add to the remaining spices in a small bowl, and mix until well blended. Set aside.

COLA RIB GLAZE

Toast the peppercorns and coriander in the bottom of a medium pot over medium heat until fragrant. Add the remaining ingredients and bring to a simmer, then cook until reduced by half, about 30 minutes. Strain out the solids with a fine-mesh strainer, return the liquid to the pot, and reduce again by half until sticky and viscous. Set aside and rewarm before serving.

TO FINISH

Dredge the ribs with the rib dry rub and let sit overnight. Preheat the broiler to high. Toast each side of the ribs with the broiler until caramelized and brown, approximately 10 minutes total. Set the oven to 325°F (163°C). Transfer the ribs to a 9″ x 13″ (23 x 33 cm) baking pan and add the chicken stock. It should come three-fourths of the way up the ribs. Cover with parchment paper folded over to fit the pan, then seal tightly with a double layer of foil and cook for 1½ to 2 hours. The meat should be almost fall-off-the-bone tender. Let cool in the broth and then remove and cut into individual ribs. Preheat the oil in a deep fryer or on the stovetop in a large pan to 375°F (191°C). Fry the ribs 3 at a time until brown, then immediately toss each batch in the warm cola rib glaze. Top with the roasted peanuts and garnish with micro mizuna and lemon zest.

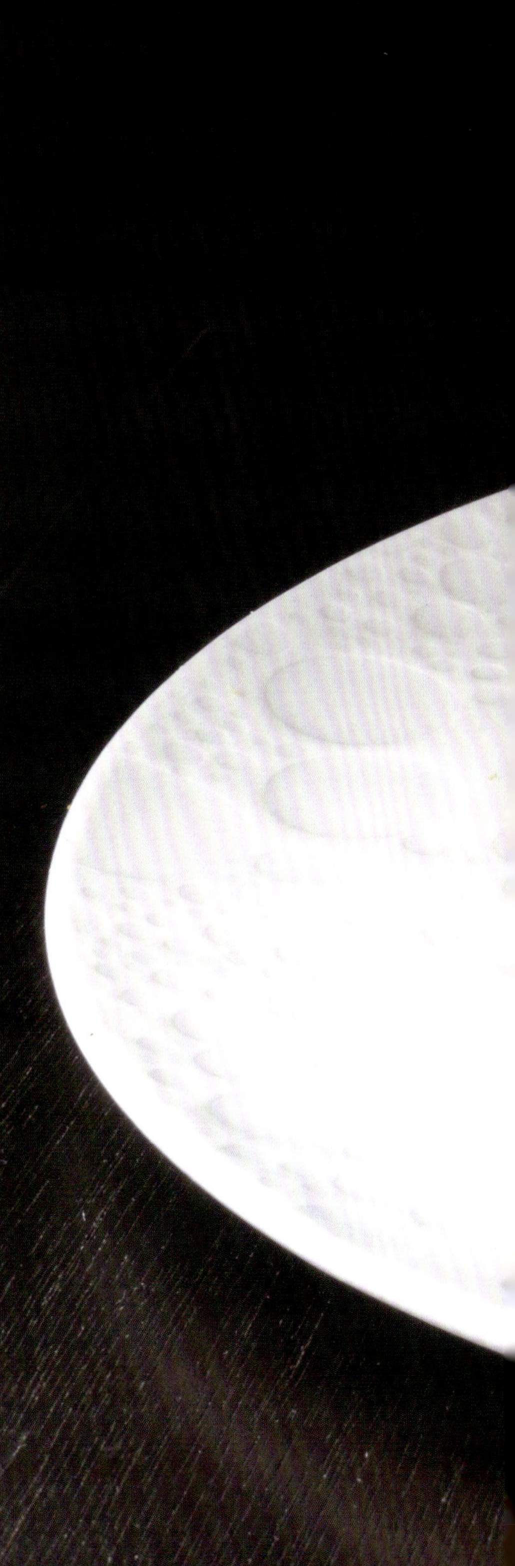

LAMB SHOULDER WITH MINT CHERMOULA

Chermoula is a North African sauce that brings a harmony of spices and herbs and helps make this dish pop. Roasted lamb can be a polarizing dish, and this recipe gives enough backbone of flavor to impress the pickiest of eaters. Lots of the gamey flavor in lamb is roasted out over the long braise, and the bright supporting flavors in the vegetables and mint chermoula balance the caramelized exterior. This lamb is Sunday-lunch approved!

SERVES 2

MACROS PER SERVING

Net carbs: 6 grams
Protein: 32 grams
Fat: 44 grams
Calories: 548

MINT CHERMOULA

1 teaspoon coriander seed
1 teaspoon cumin seed
3 cloves garlic
½ cup (118 milliliters) olive oil
½ cup (20 grams) parsley leaves
½ cup (46 grams) mint leaves
½ cup (8 grams) cilantro leaves
2 teaspoons chopped ginger
1 teaspoon Aleppo pepper
Zest and juice of 1 lemon
Salt and pepper

LAMB SPICE

1 tablespoon coriander seed
2 teaspoons cumin seed
1 teaspoon black peppercorns
1 teaspoon white peppercorns
1 tablespoon salt
2 teaspoons garlic powder
1 teaspoon dried thyme
½ teaspoon ground cloves
¼ teaspoon cinnamon
¼ teaspoon cayenne pepper

TO ASSEMBLE

½ pound (227 grams) lamb shoulder
2 tablespoons lamb spice
2 roasted red bell peppers, sliced
4 cherry tomatoes, halved
½ cup (52 grams) diced cucumber
1 tablespoon olive oil
Squeeze of lemon juice
Salt and pepper
2 tablespoons mint chermoula
Sweet alyssum flowers and red-veined sorrel, for garnish

MINT CHERMOULA

In a small skillet over medium heat, toast the coriander and cumin seeds until fragrant. Grind and add to a high-powered blender with the remaining ingredients. Blend until smooth. Set aside.

LAMB SPICE

In a small skillet over medium heat, toast the coriander and cumin seeds and both peppercorns until fragrant. Grind, add to the remaining spices in a small bowl, and mix until well blended.

TO ASSEMBLE

Rub the lamb shoulder with 2 tablespoons of the lamb spice and let sit overnight in the fridge. Preheat the oven to 375°F (191°C). Place the lamb in a roasting pan and roast, uncovered, for 25 minutes and then reduce the temperature to 275°F (135°C) and continue to roast for 2 hours, or until the meat reaches an internal temperature of 200°F (93°C). Let rest for 30 minutes and then slice. Toss the roasted peppers, tomatoes, and cucumbers in the olive oil, lemon juice, salt, and pepper. Serve the sliced lamb shoulder atop the vegetables. Drizzle with the mint chermoula and garnish with the sweet alyssum flowers and red-veined sorrel.

SERVES 2

MACROS PER SERVING

Net carbs: 9 grams
Protein: 41 grams
Fat: 31 grams
Calories: 479

GRILLED CHICKEN CAESAR

Caesar dressing is the perfect harmony of aggressively satiating flavors. I have made Caesars in eclectic variations over the years, all stemming from the original recipe created by chef Caesar Cardini. But I feel like I finally perfected my understanding of this classic by realizing that every element in the dressing is used to cut through the flavors of the opposing ingredients, creating a perfect balance. The bite of garlic is tempered by the floral quality of the lemon juice. Parmesan adds body and stability to the intensity of the anchovies. And the vinegar gives life to the olive oil, which calms the cacophony of flavors. There is a reason Caesar salad is a staple on every menu across the world, and that is because it brings umami, sour, salt, and spice. Keep this dressing in your fridge at all times to allow for a quick snack or an impromptu side. I like making this dish with airline chicken breast, a cut with the wing bone still attached. A bone-in breast means juicier, more flavorful meat—as well as a more elegant presentation.

CAESAR DRESSING

- 2 egg yolks
- 2 tablespoons microplaned garlic
- 2 tablespoons rinsed and chopped anchovies
- 2 teaspoons lemon juice
- 1 cup (237 milliliters) olive oil
- 1½ cups (120 grams) microplaned Parmesan
- 2 tablespoons red wine vinegar
- 2 tablespoons water
- 1 tablespoon fish sauce
- 2 teaspoons lemon zest
- 2 teaspoons ground black pepper
- 1 teaspoon salt

TO ASSEMBLE

- 2 airline chicken breasts
- Salt and pepper
- 6 tablespoons microplaned Parmesan
- 1 tablespoon canola oil
- Oil, for frying (such as canola, bran, or peanut oil)
- 20 parsley leaves
- 2 tablespoons microplaned aged Gouda (such as Beemster)
- 2 hearts romaine, sliced lengthwise into spears
- ¼ cup (59 milliliters) Caesar dressing
- Pea flowers, for garnish

CAESAR DRESSING

Blend the egg yolks, garlic, anchovies, and lemon juice in a high-powered blender for 3 minutes. Slowly add all the oil over 1 minute, then add all the remaining ingredients and blend until fully combined. Set aside.

TO ASSEMBLE

Season the chicken with salt and pepper and let sit for 30 minutes. Meanwhile, preheat the oven to 350°F (177°C) and sprinkle about three-fourths of the Parmesan cheese on a parchment-lined baking sheet in a single layer. Bake for 10 minutes until completely bubbling and allow to cool. Crumble and set aside. Leave oven on. In a large cast-iron pan, sear the chicken in the canola oil over medium-high heat, skin side down, until golden brown, about 4 minutes. Flip the chicken and finish cooking in the oven for about 10 minutes, or until the internal temperature reaches 165°F (74°C). Remove from the oven and let rest for 5 minutes before serving. Meanwhile, heat a deep fryer or a large pan with about 2" (5 cm) of oil to 350°F (177°C) and fry the parsley leaves until crispy and no more bubbles form. Remove onto a paper towel. Sprinkle the Gouda over the top of the chicken breasts. Toss the romaine in the dressing and arrange around the chicken. Garnish with crumbled baked Parmesan, fried parsley leaves, and pea flowers.

SEARED OCTOPUS WITH PERI-PERI DRESSING AND CAULIFLOWER AIOLI

SERVES 2

MACROS PER SERVING

Net carbs: 11 grams
Protein: 43 grams
Fat: 54 grams
Calories: 502

In Hawaii, octopus (tako) is plentiful and widely available but rarely cooked to tender perfection. The sous vide process makes the octopus melt in your mouth, while the extra crisping in the cast-iron gives a contrast of texture. I have a bag of cooked octopus in my freezer at all times as it holds up very well and tenderizes further when frozen. My peri-peri dressing is simple and effective at cutting through the savory elements of the dish.

SOUS VIDE OCTOPUS

5 octopus tentacles
¼ cup (59 milliliters) olive oil
8 cloves garlic
5 sprigs thyme
1½ teaspoons salt
1½ teaspoons pepper

CAULIFLOWER AIOLI

1 quart (946 milliliters) canola oil
4 tablespoons chopped garlic (6 to 7 cloves)
½ cup (54 grams) chopped cauliflower
3 egg yolks
1 tablespoon lemon juice
2 teaspoons salt
1 teaspoon ground white pepper
1 teaspoon lemon zest

PERI-PERI DRESSING

1 roasted red bell pepper
3 cloves garlic, minced
¼ cup (59 milliliters) canola oil
3 tablespoons chopped Thai (bird's eye) chilies
2 tablespoons champagne vinegar
1 tablespoon lemon juice
2 teaspoons salt
1½ teaspoons smoked paprika
1 teaspoon ground white pepper
1 teaspoon dried oregano
Zest and juice of 1 lemon

TO ASSEMBLE

Sous vide octopus tentacles
1 tablespoon canola oil
2 green onions
Oil, for frying (such as canola, bran, or peanut oil)
8 brussels sprouts
Pinch of salt
½ cup (118 milliliters) cauliflower aioli
6 tablespoons peri-peri dressing
4 ounces (113 grams) aged Gouda (such as Beemster), thinly sliced
Micro dill, for garnish

SOUS VIDE OCTOPUS

Bring a large pot of water to boil and set a sous vide immersion circulator to 190°F (88°C). Blanch the octopus in boiling water for 1 minute, then plunge into an ice bath. Once fully cool, add the octopus to a plastic water-resistant bag along with the olive oil, garlic, thyme, salt, and pepper. Close the bag securely or vacuum seal, then add to the sous vide immersion bath. Reduce the temperature to 174°F (79°C) and cook for 4 hours. Remove from the water and plunge into an ice bath. Remove the octopus from the bag after it has cooled, about 10 minutes, and move the octopus to a covered container in the fridge until ready to use.

CAULIFLOWER AIOLI

In a medium saucepan over low heat, bring the oil and garlic to a simmer for 10 minutes, then turn off the heat and let sit for 30 minutes. Strain out the garlic and set aside, then remove the oil to the fridge to chill. Bring a large pot of water to boil and season with salt. Cook the cauliflower for 10 minutes until it is very soft. Strain and cool. In a food processor, blend the yolks for 5 minutes until opaque. Add the cooked garlic and cauliflower and continue to blend. With the food processor running, add the cooled garlic oil slowly until the mixture begins to thicken. Once three-fourths of the oil has been added, add the lemon juice, salt, pepper, and lemon zest. Add the remaining oil and blend until homogenized. Taste for seasoning.

PERI-PERI DRESSING

Mix all the ingredients in a blender until homogeneous and emulsified.

TO ASSEMBLE

In a large cast-iron pan over medium-high heat, sear the sous vide octopus in the canola oil until crispy on both sides, about 4 minutes total. Set the octopus aside and sear the green onions in the same pan until browned. Heat a deep fryer or a pot of oil to 350° (177°) and fry the brussels sprouts until crispy and browned, then toss them in the salt. To plate, wrap the tentacles around the fried brussels sprouts and seared green onions, pipe the aioli around the dish, and spoon the dressing over the top. Garnish with the Gouda and micro dill.

PANCETTA DEVILED EGG SALAD

Egg salad is good on its own, but once you add crispy bacon bits and pancetta, it gets taken to the next level. The richness of the egg mixture is coupled with a salad full of herbaceousness and acidity. The basil aioli is essentially a vegan coulis, or a vegetable puree, mixed with an aioli to give the brightness of quickly blanched herbs with the stability of an egg emulsion. The fried capers add a bit of crunch and salinity back into the dish in case the egg mix isn't in every bite.

SERVES 3

MACROS PER SERVING

Net carbs: 3 grams
Protein: 27 grams
Fat: 45 grams
Calories: 525

BASIL AIOLI

1 cup (24 grams) basil leaves
1 cup (40 grams) parsley leaves
3 tablespoons water
3 tablespoons olive oil
1/16 teaspoon (¼ of ¼ teaspoon) xanthan gum
2 tablespoons white pepper aioli (page 58)
Salt and pepper

PANCETTA DEVILED EGGS

4 tablespoons chopped pancetta
¼ cup (59 milliliters) water
4 hard-boiled eggs, chopped
2 tablespoons white pepper aioli (page 58)
2 teaspoons pickle brine
2 teaspoons lemon juice
1 teaspoon mustard powder
3 slices crispy cooked bacon, chopped

TO ASSEMBLE

3 tablespoons capers, rinsed and drained
¼ cup (59 milliliters) oil, for frying (such as canola, bran, or peanut oil)
6 baby heads of lettuce, leaves roughly torn
3 cups (60 grams) heirloom arugula
6 tablespoons shaved celery
6 squash blossoms, separated into individual petals
2 tablespoons olive oil
2 tablespoons lemon juice
Salt and pepper
¾ cup (167 grams) pancetta deviled eggs
3 tablespoons basil aioli

BASIL AIOLI

Bring a large pot of water to boil and blanch the basil and parsley for 30 seconds and then plunge them into an ice bath. Strain and blend with the 3 tablespoons of water in a high-powered blender until smooth. Add the olive oil and xanthan gum and blend. Remove from the blender and hand-whisk the mixture into the white pepper aioli, along with the salt and pepper.

PANCETTA DEVILED EGGS

In a small pan, sauté the pancetta with the water over medium heat and allow the liquid to evaporate. Cook until crispy and drain on a paper towel. In a medium bowl, mix with the remaining ingredients.

TO ASSEMBLE

In a small pan, fry the capers in the oil over medium-high heat until bubbles stop forming, then remove them and let drain on a paper towel. Toss the greens, celery, and squash blossoms with the olive oil, lemon juice, salt, and pepper, then divide the salad onto 3 plates. With 2 spoons, add a quenelle of about ¼ cup (56 grams) of the pancetta deviled eggs atop each salad, piping the basil aioli around the plates.

SERVES 3

MACROS PER SERVING

Net carbs: 5 grams
Protein: 36 grams
Fat: 43 grams
Calories: 551

GLAZED PORK

This started as an experiment to treat a pork shoulder like a short rib and turned into an original shining star of a dish. The various textures of the meat melt in the mouth while having enough of a skin to hold together and acquire a glaze during the cooking process. The spice from the sambal and the crunch from the semi-raw cabbage break down the fattiness of the succulent meat. When you braise a hunk of pork, you typically shred the meat afterward, so I find this recipe is a treat to cook because it's outside the realm of how it would be served traditionally.

PORK SPICE

- 2 tablespoons mustard seed
- 2 tablespoons black peppercorns
- 2 tablespoons coriander seed
- 2¼ teaspoons cumin seed
- 4 tablespoons smoked paprika
- 4 tablespoons salt
- 2 tablespoons chili powder
- 2 tablespoons sweet paprika
- 2 tablespoons onion powder
- 1 tablespoon garlic powder

PORK JUS

- 4 ounces (113 grams) ground pork
- 1 cup (237 milliliters) keto white wine or Shaoxing wine
- 3 quarts (2.8 liters) stock (page 64)
- 2 tablespoons Dijon mustard
- 2 tablespoons heavy cream
- 1 tablespoon fish sauce
- 1 tablespoon fennel seed
- 1 tablespoon coriander seed
- 1 tablespoon chopped garlic
- ½ bunch thyme

TO ASSEMBLE

- 1 pound (454 grams) pork shoulder, cut into 3 pieces
- 4 tablespoons pork spice
- ¼ cup (59 milliliters) pork jus
- 2 tablespoons unsalted butter
- ¾ cup (164 grams) sambal slaw (page 156)

PORK SPICE

In a small skillet over medium heat, toast the mustard seed, peppercorns, coriander seed, and cumin until fragrant. Grind, add to the remaining spices in a medium bowl, and mix until well blended.

PORK JUS

In a large pot over medium-high heat, sear the ground pork, then add the wine to deglaze the pot. Add the remaining ingredients and cook over medium heat, stirring occasionally, until reduced to 2 cups (473 milliliters), about 1 hour. Strain with a chinois or fine-mesh strainer and set aside.

TO ASSEMBLE

Cover the pork pieces in the pork spice, wrap in plastic wrap, and refrigerate overnight. Bring the meat to room temperature before cooking. Preheat the oven to 425°F (218°C). Place the pork in a roasting pan and roast, uncovered, for 45 minutes and then reduce the heat to 275°F (135°C), cover with aluminum foil, and roast an additional 2½ hours until browned and tender. Remove the pork to a cutting board to rest and strain the pan drippings into a large sauté pan. Add the pork jus and butter to the pan and cook the pan drippings mixture over medium heat until it is sticky, about 15 to 20 minutes. Add the pork to the pan and toss, glazing the meat. Turn off the heat and continue tossing to fully glaze the pork. Add the sambal slaw to each plate and top with the glazed pork.

ZUCCHINI CARBONARA

Carbonara is a dish as iconic as the Sistine Chapel, yet a stranger to many people's kitchens. I blame this on the tricky nature of tempering the eggs to effectively thicken the sauce to a rich, smooth consistency. Using a roux for a béchamel is far easier to accomplish, but there's nothing that can compare to the tender umami of the egg yolks. This recipe does not use fresh spring peas, as is customary, for the simple fact that when I was developing this recipe, Maui did not have quality peas to offer at the time. Feel free to add in any greens, pancetta, or extra yolks to suit your palate.

SERVES 2

MACROS PER SERVING

Net carbs: 5 grams
Protein: 26 grams
Fat: 67 grams
Calories: 727

CARBONARA SAUCE

½ cup (56 grams) shredded pecorino
4 tablespoons shredded Parmesan
¼ cup (59 milliliters) water
¼ cup (57 grams) unsalted butter
1 teaspoon aged sherry vinegar
1 teaspoon salt
¼ teaspoon coarsely ground black pepper
2 eggs

TO ASSEMBLE

2 zucchini
2 tablespoons olive oil, divided
4 slices prosciutto
1 cup (250 grams) carbonara sauce

CARBONARA SAUCE

In a medium saucepan over medium-low heat, cook the cheeses, water, butter, vinegar, salt, and pepper, whisking until fully combined. Remove the sauce from the heat and let cool for 5 minutes. Crack the eggs into a medium bowl. While whisking the eggs, pour 2 tablespoons of the hot cheese sauce into the bowl and continue to whisk until combined. Add 2 more tablespoons of the sauce and continue whisking. Add 2 more tablespoons the same way, then transfer the egg mixture back into the saucepan with the rest of the cheese mixture. Over low heat, carefully cook the sauce until thickened, whisking to prevent curdling. Set aside off the heat.

TO ASSEMBLE

Using either a KitchenAid vegetable sheet cutter or a mandoline, cut the zucchini into long strips. Slice ⅓" (8 mm-) wide strips with a knife to create tagliatelle-style "noodles." In a large nonstick pan with 1 tablespoon of olive oil, fry the prosciutto on medium heat just until it is crispy. Remove from the pan and set aside. Wipe out the pan and bring it back to medium heat with the remaining 1 tablespoon of olive oil, then gently sauté the zucchini for 3 minutes, or until slightly wilted. Add in the warm carbonara sauce and toss to coat for 30 seconds. Transfer to 2 bowls and top with the crispy slices of prosciutto.

TUNA NIÇOISE

Not all salads hit the spot for a full meal, but the Niçoise certainly does the job. Salade Niçoise originated in Nice, France, and is an exemplary summer delight. I like to add more herbs into the mix with an abridged green goddess dressing, which is a more recent San Franciscan creation. For this rendition, I use sashimi-grade tuna because I am blessed to be surrounded by top-notch Hawaiian yellowfin tuna on a regular basis, and it pains me to cook beautiful cuts of sashimi-grade fish when the raw preparation is so delicious. You want to use dolphin-safe canned tuna instead? Go for it.

SERVES 2

MACROS PER SERVING

Net carbs: 10 grams
Protein: 32 grams
Fat: 35 grams
Calories: 483

BROKEN GREEN GODDESS DRESSING

- ½ cup (118 milliliters) canola oil
- 3 cups (120 grams) chopped parsley leaves, divided
- 1 pint (454 grams) Greek yogurt
- 1 pint (440 grams) mayonnaise
- 1 cup (29 grams) chopped tarragon leaves
- 5 anchovies, rinsed and chopped
- 2 tablespoons lemon juice
- 1 tablespoon Dijon mustard
- 1 tablespoon fish sauce
- 1 tablespoon salt
- 2 teaspoons lemon zest
- 1 teaspoon ground white pepper

TO ASSEMBLE

- ½ pound (227 gram-) block raw tuna
- 8 jarred artichoke hearts
- 8 cherry tomatoes
- 4 green beans
- ¼ cup (60 grams) halved and pitted kalamata olives
- 1 tablespoon olive oil
- 2 teaspoons lemon juice
- Salt and pepper
- 8 baby heads of lettuce
- ½ cup (118 milliliters) broken green goddess dressing
- 10 cilantro sprigs

BROKEN GREEN GODDESS DRESSING

Blend the oil and 2 cups (80 grams) of the parsley in a high-powered blender for 5 to 10 minutes until warm, then strain through a fine-mesh strainer and set aside. In a medium bowl, mix together the remaining ingredients, including the remaining 1 cup (40 grams) of parsley. Loosely mix in the strained parsley oil so it is blended but not fully emulsified.

TO ASSEMBLE

Heat a large cast-iron pan over high heat until very hot and sear each side of the tuna for 15 seconds. Remove from the pan, let cool, and slice. In a medium bowl, toss the artichoke hearts, tomatoes, green beans, and olives with the olive oil, lemon juice, salt, and pepper. Place the baby heads of lettuce on 2 plates and layer on the vegetables, broken green goddess dressing, and tuna. Garnish with sprigs of cilantro.

PORK LARB

SERVES 2

MACROS PER SERVING

Net carbs: 13 grams
Protein: 26 grams
Fat: 43 grams
Calories: 543

Larb is the national dish of Laos, and this variation is in no way authentic, but the flavors stick to the general guidelines and still hit those powerfully balanced notes found in the original. I include the crispy garlic and shallots to add more depth while lending their crunch to substitute for traditional khao khoua (toasted rice). To me, there is nothing more satisfying than balancing a dish to temper the acute flavor of fish sauce, and the bright flavors here do that beautifully. I love to scoop up the dish with lettuce leaves. The Swerve brown sugar is a great low-carb substitute for palm sugar.

LARB DRESSING

6 tablespoons fish sauce (such as padaek)
4 tablespoons lime juice
4 tablespoons canola oil
2 tablespoons sesame oil
2 tablespoons Swerve brown sugar
2 cloves garlic
4 teaspoons minced ginger
2 teaspoons salt

TO ASSEMBLE

½ pound (227 grams) ground pork
½ cup (118 milliliters) larb dressing, divided
Salt and pepper
4 tablespoons roasted peanuts
2 tablespoons crispy shallots (page 88)
2 teaspoons store-bought crispy garlic
2 teaspoons Korean chili flakes (such as Wang brand)
1 cucumber, sliced
½ cup (46 grams) mint leaves
½ cup (8 grams) cilantro leaves
½ cup (12 grams) Thai basil leaves
2 serrano peppers, thinly sliced

LARB DRESSING

Blend all the ingredients in a high-powered blender until well combined. Set aside.

TO ASSEMBLE

Heat a large cast-iron pan over high heat until scorching hot. Add the pork, spread it out, and press down hard with a metal spatula. Cook until browned on the bottom, about 3 minutes, then flip the meat and scrape the bottom of the pan, making sure to get all the tasty brown parts off. Once the pork is fully cooked, deglaze the pan with 2 tablespoons of the larb dressing and season with salt and pepper. Remove to plates and top with the peanuts, shallots, garlic, and chili flakes. Toss the cucumber, herbs, and peppers in the remaining dressing and season with salt to taste. Layer around the larb and enjoy.

LOBSTER ROLL

I have spent significant time in Massachusetts, and I can confidently say that nearly everyone living there would denounce this version of a lobster roll. That doesn't mean it's not delicious, but this isn't a recipe for people who are subservient to the classic preparation. The flavors are a bit punchier, the bread comes in keto biscuit form, and the fried quail egg is a kicker without overpowering the dish. Just be warned: if you serve a Bostonian a lobster roll with sunflower petals as a garnish, you will probably get physically assaulted. Don't let that intimidate you from trying this! Sea beans (also known as sea asparagus, pickleweed, glasswort, and samphire) are saltwater plants.

SERVES 2

MACROS PER SERVING

Net carbs: 9 grams
Protein: 19 grams
Fat: 35 grams
Calories: 427

LOBSTER MIX

- 6 ounces (170 grams) lobster, cooked and roughly chopped
- 4 tablespoons mayonnaise
- 4 tablespoons chopped sea beans or thinly shaved celery
- 4 tablespoons chopped green onions
- 2 tablespoons capers, rinsed and drained
- 2 tablespoons minced shallots
- 2 tablespoons lemon juice
- 2 teaspoons lemon zest
- 1 teaspoon ground white pepper
- Splash of hot sauce
- Salt and pepper

TO ASSEMBLE

- 2 keto biscuits (page 22), cut, or keto bread of choice
- ¼ cup (57 grams) unsalted butter, melted
- 1 tablespoon canola oil
- 4 quail eggs
- 1 cup (182 grams) lobster mix
- ½ teaspoon ground white pepper
- 2 sunflower petals
- Sea beans, fennel fronds, and thinly sliced celery, for garnish

LOBSTER MIX

In a medium bowl, gently mix all the ingredients together until fully incorporated.

TO ASSEMBLE

Toast the biscuit (or keto bread) in a medium pan over medium-high heat until golden brown. In a medium pan, heat the canola oil over medium heat and fry the quail eggs to your liking. Pile ½ cup (91 grams) of the lobster mix onto each biscuit, add 2 fried quail eggs to each, sprinkle with the white pepper, top with a sunflower petal, and layer on the garnishes.

LOBSTER BLT

This sandwich may be a little too rich for some people, but it's easy, delicious, and enjoyable to make. Feel free to substitute a 4-ounce (113-gram) burger patty for the lobster. I just wanted to have some fun while I had lobster on hand. I find sticking to keto to be easier when I am excited about the meals I make. Sandwiches are one of my favorite foods, and really most meats and combinations work as long as the bread is keto-friendly. One of my favorites comes from Franz bakery. It keeps its structural integrity without raising a ton of suspicion that no actual grains are present. While shallow-poaching the lobster tail, the court bouillon helps incorporate complexity and heightens the mild flavors of fresh lobster. The liquid can be strained, reduced, and turned into a sauce for another dish if desired.

SERVES 2

MACROS PER SERVING

Net carbs: 10 grams
Protein: 48 grams
Fat: 70 grams
Calories: 862

WHITE PEPPER AIOLI

- 3 egg yolks
- 1 clove garlic, minced
- 2 teaspoons fish sauce
- 1 quart (946 milliliters) canola oil
- 2 teaspoons lemon juice
- 2 teaspoons ground white pepper
- 2 teaspoons salt

COURT BOUILLON

- 2 quarts (1.9 liters) fish stock
- 1 cup (237 milliliters) keto white wine
- 1 carrot, sliced
- 1 yellow onion, sliced
- 1 leek, sliced
- 1 tablespoon toasted coriander seed
- 1 tablespoon toasted black peppercorn
- 1 tablespoon fish sauce

TO ASSEMBLE

- 2 lobster tails
- 2 keto buns (such as Franz)
- 6 tablespoons white pepper aioli
- 1 avocado, sliced
- 2 slices heirloom tomato
- 2 leaves green leaf lettuce
- 6 slices cooked, crispy bacon

WHITE PEPPER AIOLI

In a medium bowl, whisk the egg yolks, garlic, and fish sauce for 5 minutes until opaque. While whisking, start to slowly add the oil. When half the oil has been added, add the lemon juice, pepper, and salt and blend. While whisking, add the remaining oil and season with more salt or lemon juice if necessary.

COURT BOUILLON

In a large pot, combine the ingredients and bring to a simmer. Continue to simmer uncovered for 30 minutes and then strain out the solids. Put the bouillon back in the pot.

TO ASSEMBLE

Bring the court bouillon back to a boil with 2 pinches of salt. Drop in the lobster tails and turn off the heat. Cook for 4½ minutes, remove the lobster tails, and then plunge them into an ice bath. Remove the shell and slice each lobster tail in half. Toast the keto buns until brown, then top with the aioli. Layer the buns with the lobster, avocado, tomato, lettuce, and bacon.

SERVES 2

MACROS PER SERVING

Net carbs: 8 grams
Protein: 14 grams
Fat: 33 grams
Calories: 385

CHILE RELLENO COLORADO

I had one of my first traditional chiles rellenos when I was ten years old at a family-owned restaurant outside of Albuquerque, New Mexico. My uncle had been a regular there for years. I remember the waiter looked to be about the same age as I was. My uncle ordered chiles rellenos for the table without conferring with anyone. I was already an avid relleno fan, as we frequented a Salvadoran fixture in the Bay Area called La Bamba. But this particular restaurant's humble presentation of this classic dish changed my perspective on chiles rellenos forever. The chili pepper was long and slender, the dough was as crispy as the batter on fish-and-chips, and the cheese was fresh and local, made just down the street. I have experimented with different batters and peppers over the years to try to re-create that satiation. The Colorado sauce for this book was supplemented with the bacon drippings that had started to take over my fridge after all my recipe testing, and the results were amazing. If you are keto-ing like I do, you probably will have a fair amount of bacon fat saved as well. The batter is simply whipped egg, which is as traditional as you can get without adding masa harina (corn flour), and the cheese is interchangeable as long as it's melty, neutral in flavor, and plentiful.

BACON-FAT SALSA COLORADO

- 2 dried ancho chilies
- 2 dried chipotle chilies
- 4 dried pasilla chilies
- 2 tablespoons chopped garlic
- 4 tablespoons bacon fat, divided
- 2 cups (473 milliliters) chicken stock
- 1 tablespoon red wine vinegar
- 1 tablespoon dried oregano
- 1 tablespoon coriander seed
- 1 teaspoon cumin seed
- 1 teaspoon salt

CHILE RELLENO

- 2 Anaheim chilies
- ½ cup (56 grams) shredded Mexican melting cheese
- 4 eggs
- 4 teaspoons cream of tartar
- 2 tablespoons almond flour
- Oil, for frying (such as canola, bran, or peanut)
- Salt and pepper

TO ASSEMBLE

- ½ cup (130 grams) bacon-fat salsa Colorado
- 2 chiles rellenos
- 4 tablespoons farmer's cheese
- Micro cilantro, for garnish

BACON-FAT SALSA COLORADO

Over an open flame or on a foil-lined tray under a broiler, toast the chilies for 30 seconds to release the essential oils, then set aside. In a medium saucepan over medium heat, sauté the garlic in 1 tablespoon of the bacon fat until fragrant and paler in color, about 2 minutes, stirring frequently and taking care not to brown. Add the chilies, chicken stock, vinegar, spices, and salt and bring to a simmer for 20 minutes. Remove from the heat and blend in a high-powered blender until smooth. Add the remaining bacon fat to the pan and heat on high heat, then add the chili puree. Be careful; it will splatter. Lower the heat to medium and cook for 10 minutes, stirring constantly to ensure it doesn't burn on the bottom, until thickened. Remove from the heat and set aside.

CHILE RELLENO

Over an open flame or on a foil-lined tray under a broiler, char the peppers until blackened and then transfer to a medium bowl and cover with plastic wrap to steam for 30 minutes. Remove the charred skin gently and cut a slit near the stem to remove the seeds. Be careful not to open the pepper too much. Once all the seeds are removed, delicately stuff with cheese. Close the slit and press firmly together. Freeze for 30 minutes. Separate the egg whites from yolks and beat the whites with the cream of tartar until stiff peaks form. Fold in the egg yolks. Remove the peppers from the freezer and dredge with the almond flour. Fill a large pan with 1″ (2.5 cm) of the oil and bring to medium-high heat. Dip each pepper in the egg batter and place in the heated oil. Once the bottom is brown, flip gently to cook evenly. Let fry over medium heat until crispy and fully cooked, 6 to 8 minutes. Drain on a paper towel and season with salt and pepper.

TO ASSEMBLE

Warm the sauce, add ¼ cup (65 grams) to each plate, and layer a crispy chile relleno on top. Garnish each with crumbled farmer's cheese and micro cilantro.

BURMESE SALAD

The star of this dish is lahpet—fermented or pickled tea leaves. Myanmar (formerly Burma) is one of the few regions where this delicacy is eaten. All the ingredients are best served freshly tossed, and this can be the centerpiece of your lunch or an accoutrement. Keeping the ingredients crunchy and fresh makes this dish a textural delight. You can typically purchase lahpet at your local Asian supermarket, but it is also available online.

SERVES 2 TO 3

MACROS PER SERVING

Net carbs: 7 grams
Protein: 5 grams
Fat: 35 grams
Calories: 363

BURMESE SALAD DRESSING

¼ cup (59 milliliters) canola oil
3 tablespoons allulose or Swerve sugar
2 tablespoons fish sauce
1 tablespoon sherry vinegar
1 tablespoon mayonnaise
1 tablespoon sesame oil
2 teaspoons sriracha
2 teaspoons soy sauce
2 teaspoons minced ginger
1 teaspoon chopped garlic
Salt and pepper

TO ASSEMBLE

1 head Chinese red cabbage (red Napa cabbage), shredded
1 cup (16 grams) cilantro leaves
4 tablespoons torn mint leaves
2 tablespoons Burmese salad dressing
Salt and pepper
2 red radishes, sliced
2 tablespoons chopped roasted peanuts
2 tablespoons chopped lahpet
1 tablespoon crispy shallots (page 88)
1 tablespoon sesame oil
Micro mustard greens and marigold petals, for garnish

BURMESE SALAD DRESSING

Add all the ingredients to a high-powered blender and blend until homogenized.

TO ASSEMBLE

Toss the cabbage, cilantro, and mint with the dressing and season with salt and pepper. Top with the remaining ingredients and serve promptly.

KITCHEN-SINK PORK RAMEN

Throwing in the "kitchen sink" refers to unloading whatever random ingredients are readily available to make a hodgepodge fusion of flavor. I feel a bit hesitant even calling this a ramen since nearly every element is nontraditional, but the result is similarly satisfying. When it comes to any soup, the stock is the component that separates the mediocre from the exceptional. This stock is packed with flavor. If you like, you can further increase the depth by simmering additional umami-rich foods like dried mushrooms, dried seafood, and kombu. Gelatin from bones is what provides the body of the soup, and the variety of meat used adds to the complexity of flavors. Drinking soups also helps with keeping hydrated, so keep this stock on hand for a good go-to lunch. Feel free to finish with soy, fish sauce, hoisin, or oyster sauce for an added flavor boost.

SERVES 2

MACROS PER SERVING

Net carbs: 15 grams
Protein: 34 grams
Fat: 56 grams
Calories: 700

STOCK

- 5 pounds (2.27 kilograms) beef bones
- 5 pounds (2.27 kilograms) pork bones
- 5 pounds (2.27 kilograms) chicken bones
- 1 head garlic
- 1 bay leaf
- 1 pound (454 grams) carrots, roughly chopped
- 1 pound (454 grams) onions, roughly chopped
- 1 pound (454 grams) celery, roughly chopped

TO ASSEMBLE

- 2 (3-ounce [85-gram]) servings pork belly confit (page 107)
- 2 medium shrimp, shelled and deveined
- 1 (7-ounce [198-gram]) pack shirataki noodles
- 1 quart (946 milliliters) stock
- 2 (6-minute) eggs
- 2 tablespoons kimchi (page 155)
- 2 baby turnips, sliced with a mandoline
- 2 green onions, sliced thin
- 2 teaspoons togarashi
- 1 teaspoon gochujang oil (page 25)

STOCK

Preheat the oven to 350°F (177°C) and roast the bones for 1 hour, then deglaze the roasting pan with about 1 cup (237 milliliters) of water. Add to a large pot with enough water to cover the bones by about 2″ (5 cm), then bring to a boil. Once boiling, dump the water, straining out the bones. Refill the pot with water and add the bones back to the pot. Bring to a simmer and cook for 10 minutes, occasionally straining the fat off the top when it forms. Cook for 4 hours, continually straining the fat and scum off the top. Add the remaining ingredients and cook for 1 more hour. Strain out the solids, return the stock to the pot, bring to a simmer, and cook until reduced by half, about 45 minutes. Cool and store in the fridge.

TO ASSEMBLE

In a medium pot over medium heat, warm the pork, shrimp, and noodles in the stock. Ladle into bowls and top with the remaining ingredients. Feel free to add any fresh keto-friendly vegetables and proteins that may be crowding up the back of your fridge.

SMALL PLATES

CHICKEN SKEWERS

Who doesn't love meat on a stick? Well, besides vegans. Humans seem to have a primordial connection to taking food and roasting it over an open fire. Using your hands to remove each piece of meat from a pointy skewer offers some kind of dangerous titillation, where punishment and reward are merely a poke away. Every culture around the world has their own version of skewered meat, and in honor of that tradition, I added one to this book. This recipe incorporates as much flavor into the chicken as possible, because taking the time to do it right makes a difference. The glaze adds the finishing caramelization that contributes to the cacophony of flavor that builds over the two-day process. Finally, I prefer to grill on binchotan, a Japanese charcoal. It provides a higher heat and is more consistent. Following this procedure is not 100 percent necessary, but it will absolutely give you the best results. The act of grilling the meat is almost as enjoyable as eating it . . . almost.

SERVES 4

MACROS PER SERVING

Net carbs: 4 grams
Protein: 35 grams
Fat: 12 grams
Calories: 256

BRINED CHICKEN

- 1½ gallons (5.7 liters) cold water
- 1½ cups (362 grams) salt
- 1 cup (96 grams) loose black tea
- ½ cup (96 grams) Swerve granular sugar
- 2 bay leaves
- 1 bunch thyme
- 1 bunch rosemary
- 2 tablespoons black peppercorns
- 2 tablespoons coriander seed
- 2 heads garlic, sliced in half
- 1 tablespoon whole allspice
- 1 tablespoon fennel seed
- 3 lemons, halved
- 1 teaspoon chili flakes
- 1½ gallons (3.8 liters) ice
- 1 pound (454 grams) boneless chicken thighs

CHICKEN MARINADE

- ¼ cup (59 milliliters) canola oil
- 2 tablespoons chopped garlic
- 1 tablespoon miso paste
- 2 teaspoons lemon zest
- 2 teaspoons ground black pepper

CHICKEN GLAZE

- 4 teaspoons sesame oil
- 2 tablespoons minced garlic
- 2 tablespoons minced ginger
- ½ cup (118 milliliters) Shaoxing wine
- ½ cup (118 milliliters) soy sauce
- 4 tablespoons sugar-free jam (such as blackberry)
- 1 tablespoon Swerve brown sugar
- 4 teaspoons sriracha

TO ASSEMBLE

- 1 pound (454 grams) marinated chicken thighs, cut into chunks
- ½ cup (118 milliliters) chicken glaze
- 1 cup (85 grams) pea tendrils
- 1 cup (150 grams) kimchi (page 155)
- 1 teaspoon Korean chili flakes (such as Wang brand)

BRINED CHICKEN

In a large pot, bring all the ingredients besides the ice and chicken to a boil and simmer for 20 minutes. Turn off the heat and let stand for 20 minutes. Place the ice into a large container, then strain the brine through a fine-mesh strainer into the ice. Once fully chilled, add the chicken. Cover, place in the fridge, and brine for 24 hours.

CHICKEN MARINADE

Remove the chicken from the brine and pat dry. In a large bowl, mix the oil, garlic, miso, lemon zest, and pepper together until well combined. Add the chicken and toss with the marinade to evenly coat. Refrigerate and let rest for at least 4 hours.

CHICKEN GLAZE

Pour the sesame oil into a small saucepan and bring to medium heat. Add the garlic and ginger, reduce the heat to medium-low, and sweat until fragrant and translucent, about 2 minutes. Pour in the wine and cook until reduced to around half the original volume, about 10 minutes. Add the remaining ingredients and continue cooking to reduce again by half. Strain out the solids and set aside.

TO ASSEMBLE

Toward the end of the marinating time, soak 8 bamboo skewers in water for 30 minutes. Remove from the water and skewer the chicken to evenly fit the skewers. Heat a grill until as hot as possible and add the chicken to the grill. Using a brush, glaze the chicken with sauce and turn multiple times until fully charred and seasoned, about 4 minutes per side. In a medium bowl, mix together the pea tendrils and kimchi and season with salt if needed. Plate the pea tendril kimchi and skewers and serve warm with a pinch of chili flakes over the top.

BEEF TARTARE

I love to challenge traditional renditions of classics because I find doing things the same way forever to be painfully boring. This hodgepodge of flavors and textures is just one way of many to showcase raw beef without masking its beautiful flavor. For the beef itself, I choose eye of round because it is lean, flavorful, manageable, and fiscally responsible. If you point your nose up at this choice, you can buy Kobe tenderloin to dice instead.

SERVES 2

MACROS PER SERVING

Net carbs: 7 grams
Protein: 50 grams
Fat: 71 grams
Calories: 867

LEMONGRASS OIL

2 stalks lemongrass, roughly chopped
1 cup (237 milliliters) olive oil

CRISPY LEEKS

1 leek
Oil, for frying (such as canola, bran, or peanut oil)

WATERCRESS WATER

1 bunch watercress
4 tablespoons parsley leaves
4 tablespoons basil leaves
1 cup (237 milliliters) ice water
1/16 teaspoon (¼ of ¼ teaspoon) xanthan gum
Salt and pepper

PUFFED SALMON SKIN

Two 4″ to 5″ (10 to 12 cm) pieces salmon skin
Oil, for frying (such as canola, bran, or peanut oil)
Salt and pepper

TO ASSEMBLE

4 ounces (113 grams) eye of round beef
1½ tablespoons brunoise-cut shallots
Salt and pepper
3 tablespoons lemongrass oil, divided
3 tablespoons crispy leeks
1 head baby green leaf lettuce, separated into leaves
2 pieces puffed salmon skin
¼ cup (59 milliliters) watercress water
Micro lemon verbena, for garnish

LEMONGRASS OIL

In a small saucepan, bring the lemongrass and oil slowly to a simmer over medium-low heat over the course of 10 minutes or so. Remove from the heat and let cool for 2 hours. Strain and store.

CRISPY LEEKS

Cut the leeks in half lengthwise, exposing the core. Remove the outer leaves and finely julienne the rest. Add about 2″ (5 cm) of oil and the leeks to a large pan, then place over medium-low heat and slowly bring the oil up to 300°F (149°C) over 15 minutes, stirring occasionally to maintain even cooking. Cook until golden brown and bubbles stop forming.

WATERCRESS WATER

Bring a large pot of water to boil. Blanch the watercress, parsley, and basil in the boiling water for 10 seconds and then remove. Add the blanched herbs to the ice water and blend in a high-powered blender with the xanthan gum for 1 minute. Pass through cheesecloth or a fine-mesh strainer and season with salt and pepper.

PUFFED SALMON SKIN

Scrape all the meat off the salmon skins to make a smooth surface. Bring a large pot of water to boil and blanch the skin for 10 seconds and remove. Prepare a food dehydrator or preheat the oven to its lowest possible setting. Place the salmon skin flat on a piece of parchment paper and dehydrate in a food dehydrator overnight or the preheated oven for 4 hours. Remove salmon skin. In a large pot, heat about 2″ (5 cm) of frying oil to 375°F (191°C). Add the salmon skin, working in batches if necessary so the skin can spread out. Once fully expanded, remove and season with salt and pepper.

TO ASSEMBLE

Cut the beef into a small dice and let sit uncovered in the fridge for 2 hours. Mix the beef with the shallots, salt, pepper, and ½ tablespoon of the lemongrass oil. Stack with the crispy leeks, baby lettuce leaves, and puffed salmon skin, then pour on the watercress water and top with the remaining lemongrass oil. Garnish with micro lemon verbena.

SERVES 2

MACROS PER SERVING

Net carbs: 10 grams
Protein: 31 grams
Fat: 63 grams
Calories: 731

LOBSTER CHAUD-FROID

Chaud-froid is an old-school sauce-preparation technique translating to "hot-cold." It is a paradoxical method of cooking in which a fresh dish is made to taste like leftovers. This version is a bit avant-garde for a typical dinner guest, but nonetheless very delicious. The style of plating seen here is more advanced for home cooks, but it is fun to meticulously arrange and makes for an entertaining challenge.

YUZU FLUID GEL

4 tablespoons yuzu concentrate
1 tablespoon water
1 teaspoon agar-agar
¼ teaspoon salt

MISO CHAUD-FROID

4 teaspoons unflavored gelatin
¼ cup (59 milliliters) whole milk
½ cup (118 milliliters) heavy cream
2 tablespoons miso paste
2 teaspoons salt
2 teaspoons lemon juice

TO ASSEMBLE

½ cup (114 grams) miso chaud-froid
½ cup (114 grams) unsalted butter, softened
4 medium watermelon radishes, sliced with a mandoline
6 medium turnips, sliced with a mandoline
2 (4-ounce [113-gram]) pieces poached lobster
4 tablespoons yuzu fluid gel
2 teaspoons Tsar Nicoulai Golden Reserve Caviar

YUZU FLUID GEL

In a small saucepan over medium heat, bring all the ingredients to a simmer. Remove, transfer to a container, and let sit in the refrigerator for 12 hours. In a high-powered blender, blend until smooth.

MISO CHAUD-FROID

In a small bowl, add the gelatin to the milk and let bloom for 10 minutes. Add the gelatin mixture to the remaining ingredients in a small saucepan. Bring to a simmer over medium heat and cook for 5 minutes, whisking constantly, until thickened. Remove from the heat, strain, and let cool to room temperature. If needed, refrigerate, covered, then bring back to room temperature before serving.

TO ASSEMBLE

Spoon the miso chaud-froid onto a plate and set aside. Lather one side of a small piece of parchment paper with butter, then layer the radish and turnip slices onto the butter-lined parchment, offsetting each piece to mimic scales. As you layer, try to create 2 rectangle shapes that will be enough to cover the 2 pieces of lobster meat. Gently lay the lobster over the vegetable slices and cut the parchment around it. Flip the whole arrangement so that the parchment is now on top. Steam the lobster in a steamer or bamboo basket, parchment side up, for 2 minutes, then remove to the prepared plate. Carefully remove the parchment, leaving the vegetable scales on top of the lobster. Using a squeeze bottle and tweezers, add the fluid gel and caviar around the plate.

BRIE TARTLET

When I am on keto, I miss my morning pastries with my coffee. This tartlet can be served at any time of day and is a surprisingly great accompaniment with seared meat or a salad. I keep extra tart dough in my freezer for when my cravings hit. Brie works best with this recipe due to its perfect moisture and fat content. Add whatever flavors or toppings you like to make this dish yours. I had a plethora of baby greens growing at Hua Momona Farms that I utilized.

MAKES 3 TARTLETS

MACROS PER SERVING

Net carbs: 3 grams
Protein: 15 grams
Fat: 20 grams
Calories: 252

¼ cup (59 milliliters) whole milk
6 ounces (170 grams) Brie, rind removed
1 teaspoon salt
1 teaspoon lemon juice
1 egg
1 egg yolk
3 parbaked keto pie crusts (page 33)
1 teaspoon Kashmiri chili powder
Micro red Russian kale, for garnish

Preheat the oven to 325°F (163°C). In a small saucepan over medium heat, bring the milk and cheese to a simmer with the salt and lemon juice. Scoop 2 tablespoons into a small bowl with the egg and egg yolk and whisk until fully combined. Add the egg mixture to the milk mixture and turn the heat down to low. Whisk and scrape the bottom of the saucepan with a spatula until thickened. Pour the mixture into the parbaked pie crusts and bake for 15 minutes, or until golden brown. Remove and let set for 4 hours in the fridge before serving, garnished with Kashmiri chili powder and microgreens.

SERVES 2 TO 4

MACROS PER SERVING

Net carbs: 4 grams
Protein: 26 grams
Fat: 25 grams
Calories: 345

SEAFOOD CHAWANMUSHI

When your neighbor goes prong-hunting for Kauai prawns and shows up at your door with five pounds of shrimp, you use it immediately in your cookbook recipes. This dish started off as a crab dish, but I happily added shrimp into the mix and used the shells to make an oil topping. Chawanmushi is a Japanese delicacy traditionally enjoyed as a light dish during a meal. It's very simple in essence. It consists of equal parts dashi and egg, which is then steamed into a perfect custard consistency. All the flavors included here are notes that can easily be substituted with an array of back-of-the-pantry sauces collecting dust. The key to keeping items suspended in the dish is either to add enough large ingredients to hold them up or to quickly add ingredients strategically during the cooking.

SHRIMP OIL

1 pint (76 grams) shrimp shells
1 quart (946 milliliters) neutral oil (such as vegetable oil)

DASHI

2 ounces (57 grams) kombu
½ cup (118 milliliters) water
2 ounces (57 grams) katsuobushi (bonito flakes)

TO ASSEMBLE

4 eggs
½ cup (118 milliliters) dashi
4 teaspoons fish sauce
2 tablespoons thinly sliced green onions
2 ounces (57 grams) crab meat
12 Kauai prawns or medium shrimp, shelled and deveined
4 tablespoons store-bought crispy garlic
2 tablespoons shrimp oil
2 teaspoons chopped cilantro
Micro pea tendrils, for garnish

SHRIMP OIL

Combine the shrimp shells and oil in a large pot and heat over low heat for about 10 minutes. Once it begins to simmer, remove from the heat and let stand for 2 hours. Strain with a fine-mesh strainer, discard the shells, and store the oil in the fridge.

DASHI

Add the kombu and water to a small saucepan and bring slowly to a simmer on low heat over about 30 minutes. Turn off the heat and add the katsuobushi. Let steep 30 minutes. Strain with a fine-mesh strainer and reserve.

TO ASSEMBLE

Thoroughly whisk the eggs, dashi, fish sauce, and green onions together. Pour the egg mixture to fill halfway up 2 to 4 ramekins (depending on their size), using about two-thirds of the mixture. Add the crab and shrimp, equally divided between the ramekins. Add more of the egg mixture to fill the ramekins and steam for 5 to 10 minutes in a steamer, depending on the dimensions of the ramekins. Chawanmushi in smaller, shallower ramekins will cook more quickly. Once the custard is set, remove the ramekins from the steamer and garnish with crispy garlic, shrimp oil, cilantro, and micro pea tendrils.

SERVES 4

MACROS PER SERVING

Net carbs: 4 grams
Protein: 35 grams
Fat: 40 grams
Calories: 561

CHICKEN WINGS

Dry-fried wings are a special delight that most people don't connote with "healthy living," but eaten in moderation, these wings can hit the spot when keto motivation begins to wane. While working at Scala's Bistro in San Francisco in 2010, I took to snacking on extra wings with Tabasco and fresh lime juice. I added an extra layer of flavor by sprinkling chicken bouillon powder on the chicken. Some consider it a cheat, but I don't care about their opinions. Speaking of which, take notice of the addition of MSG to the dressing. Be one with the MSG. The "Chinese restaurant syndrome" that gave all the initial negative press about MSG has been proven to be factually false and racist propaganda. Use it with a light hand, though, because it does have an aggressive aftertaste.

BUTTERMILK-FETA DRESSING

- ¼ cup (55 grams) mayonnaise
- ¼ cup (30 grams) sour cream
- ¼ cup (59 milliliters) buttermilk
- ¼ cup (28 grams) crumbled feta cheese
- 1 tablespoon chopped fresh dill
- 2 teaspoons onion powder
- 2 teaspoons salt
- 1 teaspoon garlic powder
- ½ teaspoon MSG

TO ASSEMBLE

- 4 tablespoons salt
- 4 teaspoons ground white pepper
- 1 pound (454 grams) chicken wings
- Oil, for frying (such as canola, bran, or peanut oil)
- ½ cup (88 grams) chicken bouillon powder
- ¼ cup (59 milliliters) fresh lime juice
- 1 teaspoon cayenne pepper
- 1 cup (237 milliliters) buttermilk-feta dressing
- Sunflower petals, for garnish

BUTTERMILK-FETA DRESSING

In a medium bowl, whisk all the ingredients together until well combined. Set aside.

TO ASSEMBLE

Preheat the oven to 350°F (177°C). Mix together the salt and white pepper. Toss the chicken wings in the salt mixture, spread out onto a baking sheet, and bake for 20 minutes, or until the internal temperature reaches 165°F (74°C). Heat a deep fryer or a large pot of oil to 375°F (191°C), then deep-fry the wings until crispy, 4 to 5 minutes. Work in batches to avoid crowding. Toss the fried wings with the chicken bouillon, lime juice, and cayenne. Pile the wings atop the dressing and garnish with sunflower petals.

CRISPY BRUSSELS WITH GARUM AND PARMESAN

Even for those who don't eat keto, this dish should be added to the year-round repertoire. The crispy texture can be achieved through a hard oven-sear at 425°F (218°C), but because I have the technology, I choose to deep-fry these suckers. Feel free to swap the pancetta with thick-cut bacon. Garum is an old ingredient used in Greek, Roman, and Phoenician cooking hundreds of years ago. It is not as common as it once was but is related to the fish sauce used widely in Southeast Asia. They are both made from fermented anchovies. For a ketolicious Thanksgiving, make this dish and serve it hot and fresh. It will overshadow any turkey—no matter how well it's been brined.

SERVES 2 TO 3

MACROS PER SERVING

Net carbs: 6 grams
Protein: 11 grams
Fat: 25 grams
Calories: 293

GARUM DRESSING

- 6 to 7 whole garlic cloves
- 1 cup (237 milliliters) grape-seed oil
- ½ cup (118 milliliters) lemon juice
- ¼ cup (59 milliliters) lime juice
- ¼ cup (59 milliliters) fish sauce
- Pinch of chili flakes
- Pinch of salt

TO ASSEMBLE

- 4 tablespoons diced pancetta
- 2 tablespoons water
- 2 cups (176 grams) halved brussels sprouts
- Oil, for frying (such as canola, bran, or peanut oil)
- 3 tablespoons garum dressing
- Salt
- 2 tablespoons microplaned Parmesan cheese

GARUM DRESSING

In a small saucepan over low heat, gently cook the garlic in the oil for 30 minutes. Cool and strain, reserving the oil and the garlic separately. When the oil and garlic have cooled, add the cooked garlic, lemon juice, lime juice, fish sauce, chili flakes, and salt to a high-powered blender and blend until smooth, then gradually add half of the cool garlic oil until emulsified. Reserve the other half for another use.

TO ASSEMBLE

In a medium pan over medium heat, sauté the pancetta and water until brown and crispy. Heat a deep fryer or a large pot of oil to 375°F (191°C) and deep-fry the brussels sprouts until dark brown and crispy. Remove to a paper-towel-lined plate to drain, then toss in a large bowl with the garum dressing, salt, and pancetta. Top with the Parmesan cheese.

TUNA POKE LETTUCE WRAPS

In Hawaii, people take their poke very seriously, and the dish has deep roots in the culture. I typically get about six to seven varieties of poke from the local liquor store, Tamura's, for a picnic with various lettuces and chips. Some of the best local Maui cuisine can be found in unassuming places. Kyurizuke are Japanese pickles that can be found near tofu in the refrigerated sections of many grocery stores. Using fresh ahi is what separates a good dish from a great dish. Get the dark-red sashimi block from the butcher shop with no blood line and have fun adding in different toppings. My favorites are kimchi furikake and crispy wakame.

SERVES 2

MACROS PER SERVING

Net carbs: 7 grams
Protein: 23 grams
Fat: 26 grams
Calories: 354

TOGARASHI AIOLI

- 1 cup (220 grams) mayonnaise
- 1 tablespoon togarashi
- 1 tablespoon lemon juice
- 1 teaspoon lemon zest
- 1 teaspoon salt
- 1 teaspoon water

POKE SAUCE

- 2 cloves garlic, minced
- 1 tablespoon minced ginger
- 2 teaspoons sesame oil
- ¼ cup (59 milliliters) soy sauce
- 2 tablespoons Swerve sugar
- 1 tablespoon sugar-free strawberry jam
- 1 teaspoon dashi powder

TO ASSEMBLE

- 6 ounces (170 grams) sushi-grade ahi, cubed
- ½ cup (65 grams) sliced onions
- ½ cup (68 grams) kyurizuke
- 6 tablespoons sliced French breakfast radishes (3 to 5 radishes)
- 4 tablespoons poke sauce
- 4 tablespoons togarashi aioli
- 4 teaspoons black sesame seed
- Micro shiso, dill, and cilantro, for garnish
- 6 baby heads of lettuce, separated into leaves

TOGARASHI AIOLI

In a small bowl, hand-whisk all the ingredients together until well combined. Set aside.

POKE SAUCE

In a small saucepan over medium heat, sauté the garlic and ginger in the sesame oil until fragrant, about 1 minute. Add the remaining ingredients and cook until thickened, about 3 minutes. Strain out and discard the solids, and reserve the sauce.

TO ASSEMBLE

Toss the fish, onions, kyurizuke, and radishes in the poke sauce and let stand for 5 minutes. Spoon into bowls and top with togarashi aioli, sesame seeds, and garnishes. Arrange the lettuces on the outside of the bowls.

FRIED TOFU

SERVES 2

MACROS PER SERVING

Net carbs: 10 grams
Protein: 28 grams
Fat: 63 grams
Calories: 719

I grew up in a vegetarian household in Northern California, so eating tofu was a weekly experience for me. As an American child, I found cold tofu to be the antithesis of delicious. But I quickly began to crave the fried version I discovered at my local Thai restaurant, Bangkok Cuisine. I always keep an array of tofus with different textures in my fridge for various uses. The soft kind is great in soups and stews or blended to use as a vegan emulsifier. The firmer varieties are wonderful pan-seared, grilled, and especially fried. This is a method referred to as dry-frying, and it takes a bit longer to achieve a very crunchy texture. Be patient and allow for the moisture to drain. Trust me, it is well worth the wait.

PEANUT SAUCE

- 3 tablespoons unsweetened smooth peanut butter
- 2 tablespoons water
- 2 teaspoons soy sauce
- 1 clove garlic, minced

TO ASSEMBLE

- 1 block firm tofu
- Oil, for frying (such as canola, bran, or peanut oil)
- Salt and pepper
- 6 tablespoons peri-peri dressing (page 44)
- 6 tablespoons peanut sauce
- ½ kohlrabi, sliced thin
- 1 bunch watercress
- Nasturtium leaves, for garnish
- ¼ cup (59 milliliters) lemon juice
- 2 teaspoons olive oil

PEANUT SAUCE

In a small bowl, whisk all the ingredients together until well blended. Set aside.

TO ASSEMBLE

Dry the tofu, then cut into a large dice. Bring a deep fryer or a large pot of oil to 350°F (177°C), then fry the tofu for 8 minutes, or until very crispy, working in batches if needed to prevent overcrowding. Remove to a paper-towel-lined plate and season with salt and pepper, then place on plates and top with the peri-peri dressing and the peanut sauce. Toss the kohlrabi, watercress, and nasturtium leaves with lemon juice and olive oil and serve alongside the tofu.

SPINACH AND ARTICHOKE DIP

While living in Massachusetts, I had a girlfriend whose parents were excellent cooks and owned a local restaurant. They loved to snack and always had a ton of dips and chips available on hand in their home. I remember first eating a creamy dip that contained water chestnuts at their house, and I lost my mind at how much crunch the water chestnuts added without imparting any flavor. This rendition is an homage to that experience in Worcester, and my time spent with that family. It's served in a hollowed-out kohlrabi because everything is better when served out of a natural vessel.

SERVES 2 TO 4

MACROS PER SERVING

Net carbs: 4 grams
Protein: 10 grams
Fat: 24 grams
Calories: 272

CRISPY PARSLEY

- 10 parsley sprigs
- Oil, for frying (such as canola, bran, or peanut oil)
- Salt

SPINACH AND ARTICHOKE DIP

- ½ pound (227 grams) cream cheese
- 1 cup (112 grams) shredded Parmesan
- 1 cup (121 grams) sour cream
- 1 cup (156 grams) frozen chopped spinach, thawed and drained
- ½ cup (130 grams) canned artichoke hearts, chopped
- 4 tablespoons water chestnuts, quartered
- 2 tablespoons thinly sliced green onions
- 1 tablespoon ranch seasoning
- 1 teaspoon lemon zest
- ½ teaspoon chili flakes
- Salt

TO ASSEMBLE

- 1 kohlrabi
- ½ cup (120 grams) spinach and artichoke dip
- 1 tablespoon crispy parsley
- 1 teaspoon Kashmiri chili powder
- 2 cucumbers, sliced

CRISPY PARSLEY

Preheat a deep fryer or a large pan with about 2″ (5 cm) of oil to 350°F (177°C), then fry the parsley until no more bubbles form, about 1 minute. Drain and season with salt to taste.

SPINACH AND ARTICHOKE DIP

In a large bowl, mix all the ingredients together, add salt to taste, and move to the fridge to chill for at least 1 hour.

TO ASSEMBLE

Hollow out the kohlrabi with a spoon and fill with the dip. Top with the crispy parsley and chili powder. Serve cucumbers alongside as crudités.

HALIBUT CRUDO

Nearly all types of fish benefit from some precursory relationship with salt. The texture improves, the fish becomes mildly seasoned, and the salt inhibits bacterial growth. The squid ink in this dish is added for visual effect and imparts very little flavor, so feel free to skip that ingredient if the occasion calls for a less dramatic presentation. Jicama gives an almost fruity characteristic to the dish but can easily be substituted with any crunchy, fresh, low-carb vegetable readily available.

SERVES 2

MACROS PER SERVING

Net carbs: 4 grams
Protein: 5 grams
Fat: 44 grams
Calories: 476

CRISPY SHALLOTS

½ cup (80 grams) shallots, sliced mandoline thin
1 quart (946 milliliters) oil, for frying (such as canola, bran, or peanut oil)
½ teaspoon salt

SQUID INK DRESSING

1 tablespoon champagne vinegar
2 teaspoons squid ink
2 teaspoons water
1 teaspoon minced shallots
1 teaspoon lemon juice
1 teaspoon soy sauce
1 teaspoon salt

CURED HALIBUT

1 tablespoon salt
1 tablespoon Swerve sugar
4 ounces (113 grams) halibut
1 tablespoon lemon zest

TO ASSEMBLE

Cured halibut, sliced thin
1 teaspoon lemon juice
Salt
2 tablespoons squid ink dressing
¼ cup (59 milliliters) olive oil
2 tablespoons crispy shallots
2 tablespoons chopped toasted Marcona almonds
2 tablespoons brunoise-cut jicama
1 tablespoon chopped chives
Micro mustard greens, for garnish

CRISPY SHALLOTS

Preheat a deep fryer or a large pan of oil to 300°F (149°C) and fry the shallots, constantly mixing until golden brown. Then quickly remove to a paper-towel-lined plate and season with the salt.

SQUID INK DRESSING

Use a high-powered blender or an immersion blender to blend all the ingredients together until smooth.

CURED HALIBUT

In a small bowl, mix together the salt and sugar. Place the fish on a plate, rub the lemon zest into it, and then cover in the salt mixture. Cure in the fridge for 4 hours and then rinse the fish with ice-cold water and pat dry.

TO ASSEMBLE

Toss the sliced halibut with the lemon juice and salt. Layer onto plates, top with the squid ink dressing, and then garnish with the remaining ingredients.

CHARCUTERIE

AVOCADO TOAST WITH CRISPY PIGS' EARS

Avocado toast is a pretty "basic bi#$h" breakfast item, so I decided to add a menagerie of supporting characters to create some depth. Pigs' ears are something you can find at a local hacienda or restaurant supply store with full-animal butchery, but don't subject yourself to your high-end butcher shop charging four times its worth. The high fat and collagen content paired with its ability to crisp firmly makes it ideal for the keto diet. Quail eggs are readily available at reasonable prices at Asian markets. Check with your local butcher as well, but they tend to charge twice the amount.

SERVES 2

MACROS PER SERVING

Net carbs: 2 grams
Protein: 22 grams
Fat: 25 grams
Calories: 321

CRISPY PIGS' EARS

2 pigs' ears
1 tablespoon coriander seed
1 teaspoon black peppercorns
5 cloves garlic
1 quart (946 milliliters) chicken stock
2 teaspoons salt
1 bay leaf
Oil, for frying (such as canola, bran, or peanut oil)

AVOCADO MASH

1 ripe avocado
2 teaspoons lime juice
Zest of 1 lime
1½ teaspoons salt
1 tablespoon brunoise-cut shallots, rinsed and dried
2 teaspoons minced cilantro

TO ASSEMBLE

2 slices keto bread
6 tablespoons avocado mash
2 quail eggs
1 tablespoon white vinegar
2 crispy pigs' ears, sliced
1 tablespoon store-bought crispy garlic
4 teaspoons Tsar Nicoulai Classic Caviar
Micro mustard greens, for garnish

CRISPY PIGS' EARS

Preheat the oven to 325°F (163°C). Make sure the pigs' ears are free of all hair. If there is any visible hair, burn it off over an open flame. Toast the coriander seed and peppercorns in a dry pan over medium heat until they are fragrant. Add the toasted spices and all the remaining ingredients except the oil to an oven-safe container that is small enough to fully submerge the ears in the stock. Cook for 3½ hours. You should be able to puncture the ears fully and easily with a fork. Remove the ears and save the liquid for other uses, like a stew or sauce. Line a terrine mold or loaf pan with parchment paper. Add the warm pigs' ears and cover with parchment. Press with a weight and refrigerate overnight, then julienne. Heat a deep fryer or a large pan of oil over medium-high heat to 350° (177°C) and fry the ears until there are only small bubbles forming, 2 to 3 minutes. Remove the ears to a paper-towel-lined plate and salt to taste.

AVOCADO MASH

In a small bowl, mix the avocado, lime juice, lime zest, and salt together and mash with a fork until blended but still somewhat chunky. Once the desired texture is reached, mix in the shallots and cilantro.

TO ASSEMBLE

Toast the bread until crispy. Top the warm toasts with the avocado mash. Poach the quail eggs for 50 seconds in water spiked with the vinegar. Top the avocado toasts with strips of crispy pigs' ear and a poached egg. Break the yolk open and garnish with crispy garlic, caviar, and micro mustard greens.

SERVES 4

MACROS PER SERVING

Net carbs: 1 gram
Protein: 11 grams
Fat: 60 grams
Calories: 588

BREAKFAST SAUSAGE

Making your own sausage may be overkill because a variety of keto-friendly brands are available. But I just love making sausage. The snap from a freshly smoked sausage is hard to beat. Pork belly is a great meat to use because it is naturally high in fat. Keep all the equipment for the stuffer and grinder cold to make sure the fat retains its integrity. I like using lamb casings to stretch out the calories and the meat farce. Breakfast links are one of the many joys in life. Have some fun with the recipe and add different spices, herbs, and even cheese.

1 pound (454 grams) ground pork belly
4 cloves garlic, microplaned
2 teaspoons salt
1½ teaspoons chopped fresh sage
1½ teaspoons Swerve sugar
1 teaspoon ground black pepper
½ teaspoon ground fennel
¼ teaspoon lemon zest
¼ teaspoon TCM no. 1 salt (see Tip)
Pinch of ground cloves
Lamb casing

Make sure all the meat is kept cold during the process of mixing and forming. Blend all the ingredients except the casing in a stand mixer with a paddle attachment until combined and homogeneous—but do not overmix. Remove to the fridge for about 30 minutes to chill before continuing. Add the farce to the stand mixer's sausage stuffer and pipe into the lamb casing, twisting the links off as you go. Keep the links cold by placing them over a metal tray filled with ice as you complete them. Hang the links in the fridge for 2 days to let them cure. When you're ready to eat them, either boil them for 10 minutes and sear them in a cast-iron skillet until fully cooked, or smoke them at 225°F (107°C) for 1½ hours until they reach an internal temperature of 165°F (74°C). I prefer the smoking process.

TIP: This recipe uses TCM (tinted curing mix) no. 1 salt, which is a salt mixed with sodium nitrite that should be used with extreme caution. It is a preservative used for slowing bacterial growth and preventing botulism. It is very useful in charcuterie but can be poisonous if ratios are not followed precisely

FOIE GRAS TORCHON WITH BRIOCHE

SERVES 6

MACROS PER SERVING

Net carbs: 7 grams
Protein: 31 grams
Fat: 26 grams
Calories: 386

Not many people can boast about losing weight while indulging in foie gras. People have reservations about the ethics behind using this product, and I support their convictions, but I also support ethical farms like Hudson Valley. Many charcuterie butchers have various forms of foie gras available, but they tend to use sweet wines to cure and wash the liver, and this will kick you out of ketosis, so buyer beware. I decided to add some spirulina at the last minute to impart some character to the dish. It is mostly flavorless and meant for aesthetics. I cannot claim that I created this brioche recipe myself. Rather, after many tests, I found a fantastic source online from Fat Kitchen that I adapted. It worked better than anything I could ever have created in my kitchen. Kudos, Charisse. Note that this recipe contains TCM no. 1 salt. See the Tip on page 95 for more on using that ingredient safely. If you can't find lupin flour locally, you can order it online.

BRIOCHE

- 1 teaspoon active dry yeast
- 1 cup (237 milliliters) water at 95°F (35°C)
- 3 tablespoons allulose
- 2 teaspoons honey
- 2 eggs
- 1¼ cups (180 grams) vital wheat gluten
- ¾ cup (98 grams) lupin flour
- ½ cup (50 grams) oat fiber
- 1½ teaspoons salt
- 2 tablespoons unsalted butter, divided
- 2 tablespoons heavy cream or egg wash (made with 1 beaten egg and a splash of water)

FOIE GRAS TORCHON

- 1 pound (454 grams) grade A foie gras chunks
- 2 tablespoons salt
- 1 tablespoon Swerve sugar
- 2 teaspoons TCM no. 1 salt
- 1 teaspoon ground white pepper
- 2 tablespoons spirulina

TO ASSEMBLE

- 12 ounces (340 grams) foie gras torchon
- Sweet alyssum flowers, for garnish
- 6 brioche buns
- 6 tablespoons sugar-free strawberry jam

BRIOCHE

In a small bowl, combine the yeast and hot water with the allulose and honey and let sit for 10 minutes. Whisk in the eggs and transfer to a stand mixer fitted with a hook attachment. In a medium bowl, mix the wheat gluten, lupin flour, oat fiber, and salt together, then add half to the mixer. Mix on medium for 3 to 4 minutes before adding the other half of the dry ingredients. Mix for 10 minutes, or until the dough becomes elastic. Add 1 tablespoon of the butter to the dough, and once fully incorporated, add the other tablespoon, mixing again until combined. Cover the bowl with a wet towel and let sit for 30 minutes. On a lightly floured surface, cut the dough and shape into 6 equal balls, move to a parchment-lined baking sheet, cover, and let rise for 90 minutes. Close to the end of the rising time, preheat the oven to 375°F (191°C). Brush the risen brioche with the cream or egg wash and bake for 20 minutes, or until golden brown. Remove and let cool on a wire rack.

FOIE GRAS TORCHON

To remove the veins of the foie gras, bring to room temperature and, using fish tweezers, follow the crevices to remove the blood lines, which are easily felt by touch. After it is completely deveined, lay 2 pieces of cheese cloth on top of each other. In a small bowl, mix the salt, sugar, TCM, and pepper together. Sprinkle half of the cure evenly over the layered cheese cloth, add the foie gras, and press and shape to form into a rectangle, about 8″ x 6″ (20 x 15 cm). Add the remaining cure over the top evenly. Let sit for 10 minutes. Sprinkle the spirulina evenly over the foie gras and then break a 2″ (5 cm-) wide piece off the long end of the foie gras and stack it on top of the larger piece. Roll the foie gras in the cheese cloth into a very tight cylinder and twist the ends to ensure it is stiff. Use another piece of cheese cloth and repeat the rolling process, making sure the ends are tight. Tie off with butcher's twine. Hang in your fridge for 3 days. The evening before you are ready to eat, bring a large pot of water to a rapid boil and then turn off the heat. Drop the torchon into the water, and let sit for 1½ minutes. Remove and plunge into ice water for 20 minutes. Transfer to the fridge and let chill for 12 hours. Unwrap the cheese cloth and re-wrap the torchon in plastic wrap, storing in the fridge until ready to serve.

TO ASSEMBLE

To serve, remove the plastic wrap and slice the torchon, garnish with sweet alyssum flowers, and serve alongside a bun and jam.

LAVENDER SALMON LOMI LOMI WITH MAC NUT STREUSEL

Lomi lomi is a Hawaiian dish typically served with tomatoes and other ingredients that were introduced by early Western settlers. Traditionally served at luaus, the salmon is salted, massaged, and shredded. This variation brings in a bit more of a Western influence. This dish was created at the request of the Ali'i Kula Lavender Farm. I enjoy spooning some of the dashi with the fish in each bite, and I sometimes add greens into the mix to make this more of a salad. It's a stunning starter that satiates without dominating the meal.

SERVES 2

MACROS PER SERVING

Net carbs: 8 grams
Protein: 31 grams
Fat: 12 grams
Calories: 264

LAVENDER-CURED SALMON

½ cup (120 grams) salt
2 tablespoons dried lavender
2 tablespoons Swerve sugar
½ salmon loin (about 1 pound [454 grams])

MAC NUT STREUSEL

2 tablespoons macadamia nuts
Zest of 1 lemon
1 tablespoon store-bought crispy onions or crispy shallots (page 88)
1 tablespoon store-bought crispy garlic
1 tablespoon roughly chopped basil leaves
8 fresh lavender blossoms

HIBISCUS DASHI

1 sheet kombu
1 quart (946 milliliters) cold water
4 tablespoons dried hibiscus blossoms
2 tablespoons katsuobushi (bonito flakes)
2 teaspoons salt

TO ASSEMBLE

6 ounces (170 grams) lavender-cured salmon, diced small
1 bulb fennel, shaved
¼ cup (59 milliliters) lemon juice
2 teaspoons olive oil
Salt and pepper
4 tablespoons mac nut streusel
½ cup (118 milliliters) hibiscus dashi
Lavender blossoms, for garnish

LAVENDER-CURED SALMON

In a spice grinder or with a mortar and pestle, grind the salt, dried lavender, and Swerve together into a fine powder. Add the mix to the salmon and coat the entire fish. Wrap in plastic wrap, place on a baking tray in the fridge, and top with a plate to apply pressure, turning it over once a day for 2 full days. Unwrap, wash in cool water, and let sit for at least 6 hours in the fridge uncovered before serving.

MAC NUT STREUSEL

Preheat the oven to 350°F (177°C). In a small pan over medium heat, toast the macadamia nuts for 5 to 10 minutes until golden brown, watching them closely so they don't burn. Cool and pulse in a food processor with the lemon zest, crispy onions, and crispy garlic until well combined. Toss with the basil leaves and lavender blossoms.

HIBISCUS DASHI

In a large saucepan, add the kombu to the cold water and gently bring it to 180°F (82°C). Steep at this temperature for 20 minutes. Turn off the heat and add the dried hibiscus and katsuobushi. Steep for 20 minutes, then strain out the solids. Season the dashi with salt and cool.

TO ASSEMBLE

Toss the diced salmon with the fennel, lemon juice, olive oil, salt, and pepper. Mold onto plates using a metal ring. Remove the metal ring, top with the mac nut streusel, and gently pour in the dashi to fill the plates. Garnish with lavender blossoms.

SALMON BLINIS

MAKES ABOUT 12 BLINIS

MACROS PER SERVING

Net carbs: 2 grams
Protein: 12 grams
Fat: 30 grams
Calories: 326

If you are unfamiliar with blinis, do not fret or be intimidated! This sophisticated pancake does not necessarily require an actual blini pan. Though if uniformity and tradition are important to you, then by all means invest in a cast-iron blini pan, as the final crunch cannot be beaten. I personally love a good silver dollar pancake, and this recipe satisfies that craving with whatever toppings I choose. Top with a poached egg and some hollandaise sauce, and you have yourself quite the breakfast. But for a crowd-pleasing appetizer, serving the blinis with salmon and its own roe builds layers of complexity, while the preserved lemon cuts the almost too-rich natural fattiness from all the omega-3s. Curing fish is nearly always better than not, and I'm happy to say that the Swerve brine keeps the flavors optimal and the texture outrageous. Cured salmon can be stored in the refrigerator, covered, for three to five days. This recipe makes far more cured salmon than you will need for the blinis, but it's so delicious you won't be sorry to have it on hand.

PRESERVED LEMON CREAM CHEESE

½ cup (121 grams) cream cheese
2 tablespoons heavy cream
2 teaspoons minced preserved lemon
1 teaspoon lemon juice
½ teaspoon salt

SWERVE-CURED SALMON

¼ cup (60 grams) salt
2 tablespoons Swerve sugar
1 tablespoon crushed coriander seed
1 tablespoon crushed fennel seed
1 tablespoon crushed mustard seed
1 teaspoon chili flakes
1 (4-pound [1.8-kilogram]) salmon loin
1 ounce (30 milliliters) keto white wine, gin, or vodka

BLINIS

2 eggs, separated
¼ cup (60 grams) cream cheese
1 tablespoon whole milk
⅔ cup (64 grams) almond flour
2 teaspoons Swerve sugar
Pinch of salt
Pinch of cayenne pepper
Canola oil or ghee to cook

TO ASSEMBLE

2 tablespoons salmon roe (ikura)
3 tablespoons extra-virgin olive oil
6 tablespoons preserved lemon cream cheese
Blinis
1 tablespoon chopped chives
3 ounces (85 grams) cured salmon, sliced thin
Chervil, for garnish

PRESERVED LEMON CREAM CHEESE

In a large bowl, use an electric mixer to combine all the ingredients until light and fluffy.

SWERVE-CURED SALMON

In a spice grinder or mortar and pestle, grind the salt, sugar, and spices together until well incorporated. Delicately wash the salmon with the alcohol, then pat dry with a paper towel. Generously sprinkle three-fourths of the salt mixture evenly on the flesh side of the fish. Turn the fish over and season the skin side with the remaining mixture. Wrap in cheesecloth or loose plastic wrap. Store on a baking sheet in the fridge with a weight on top of it, evenly dispersing the pressure. Flip the fillet every 12 hours for 2 days, making sure to drain any liquid residue. After 48 hours of curing, wash the salmon with ice water to remove the brine, and let it dry uncovered in the fridge for another 12 hours.

BLINIS

In a high-powered blender, blend the egg yolks, cream cheese, and milk until smooth. In a large bowl, whisk the flour, sugar, salt, and cayenne pepper together. Whisk the wet ingredients into the dry ingredients and let stand for 5 minutes. Meanwhile, beat the egg whites until stiff peaks form. Fold the whites into the batter one-third at a time. Heat a large pan over medium-high heat and add canola oil or ghee to fill halfway up the pan. Carefully drop 2-ounce (59-milliliter) portions of the batter (about ¼ cup) into the pan and allow to brown, 1 to 2 minutes. Use a spatula to ensure the blinis don't stick. Flip the blinis over and cook the other side equally. Place cooked blinis on a paper-towel-lined plate to remove excess grease.

TO ASSEMBLE

Gently toss the ikura in the extra-virgin olive oil and keep it cool in the refrigerator. Using a piping bag or a spoon, add dollops of the preserved lemon cream cheese on top of the warm blinis. Lightly sprinkle the chives and place a slice of the salmon on top, finishing with a healthy spoonful of ikura and chervil for garnish.

SERVES 4

MACROS PER SERVING

Net carbs: 4 grams
Protein: 20 grams
Fat: 45 grams
Calories: 501

CHICKEN LIVER MOUSSE

This foolproof method creates a delightfully light mousse that can be easily spooned onto any crunchy accoutrements. TCM no. 1 salt is being used again, so be careful to stick to the ratios and keep the pink salt properly labeled and away from someone who might confuse the curing salt with pink Himalayan salt (see Tip on page 95). I probably don't need to say this, but for the love of all that is holy, use a sharp knife when cutting chives! They wilt more easily than other herbs and are less forgiving with a dull blade.

CHICKEN LIVER MOUSSE

- About 10 large chicken livers
- 1 cup (237 milliliters) whole milk
- 2 tablespoons canola oil
- 2 tablespoons diced pancetta
- 1 tablespoon minced shallots
- ¼ cup (59 milliliters) keto white wine
- 2 eggs
- Leaves from 3 sprigs thyme
- 2 tablespoons heavy cream
- 2 tablespoons unsalted butter, melted
- 2 teaspoons salt
- 1 teaspoon ground black pepper
- 1 teaspoon TCM no. 1 salt

TO ASSEMBLE

- 4 slices keto bread
- ¼ cup (57 grams) unsalted butter, melted
- 1 cup (208 grams) chicken liver mousse
- 4 tablespoons chopped chives

CHICKEN LIVER MOUSSE

Soak the livers in the milk in the fridge for at least 4 hours and up to 1 day. Drain the milk and, over high heat, get a large cast-iron pan scorching hot. Add the canola oil and quickly sear the outside of the livers to brown them while still keeping the center raw. Remove the livers from the pan. Reduce heat to medium-low and sweat the pancetta and shallots until the shallots are translucent, about 3 minutes. Deglaze the pan with the wine and cook until thickened, then strain and discard solids. Blend the seared livers with the remaining ingredients in a blender until emulsified and strain with a fine-mesh strainer into a vacuum-seal bag. Set a sous vide immersion circulator to 154°F (68°C), then cook sous vide for 90 minutes. Remove the mixture from the bag, blend again, and transfer to a piping bag or a ziplock bag with the corner cut. Let cool for at least 4 hours.

TO ASSEMBLE

Toast the keto bread until golden brown and brush with the melted butter. Once cooled for 1 minute, pipe on the mousse. Top with the chives.

PIGS' EAR TERRINE WITH PANCETTA CHILI CRISP

I understand that the idea of pigs' ears might freak you out. When the notion of eating the offal (organs and extraneous bits) of pigs was first presented to me in high school, I felt similarly apprehensive. After exploring full-animal butchery and eating dishes where this art form is respected, I now find tails, ears, and chicharrones a must-order item on menus. They are unctuous, flavorful, and texturally satisfying. This terrine really shines with the crispy, spicy addition of the pancetta chili crisp. It was inspired by XO sauce, but is less fragrant and labor intensive. Keith and I ate the entire terrine in two days, snacking on slices in between making other dishes.

SERVES 2

MACROS PER SERVING

Net carbs: 1 gram
Protein: 13 grams
Fat: 34 grams
Calories: 362

PANCETTA CHILI CRISP

- 3 ounces (85 grams) dried scallops
- 2 cups (473 milliliters) canola oil, divided
- 3 ounces (85 grams) pancetta
- 1 cup (237 milliliters) stock (page 64)
- 4 tablespoons chili flakes
- 3 tablespoons store-bought crispy garlic
- 3 tablespoons crispy shallots (page 88)
- 2 tablespoons fish sauce
- 2 teaspoons ground Szechuan peppercorns
- 2 teaspoons dark soy sauce

PIGS' EAR TERRINE

- 2 pigs' ears
- 2 tablespoons coriander seed
- 1 teaspoon black peppercorns
- 1 quart (946 milliliters) stock (page 64)
- 5 cloves garlic
- 2 teaspoons salt
- 1 bay leaf

TO ASSEMBLE

- ½ pound (227 grams) pigs' ear terrine
- 6 tablespoons pancetta chili crisp
- Micro cilantro, for garnish

PANCETTA CHILI CRISP

In a small bowl, pour boiling water over the scallops and let sit for 1 hour to rehydrate, then drain the water and shred the scallops. In a large pot over medium heat, sauté the shredded scallops in 2 tablespoons of the canola oil until crispy, about 5 minutes, then remove from the pot. Add the pancetta and stock and bring to a simmer, cooking until the stock has evaporated and the pancetta is crispy. Add the rest of the oil and the remaining ingredients, cook over low heat for 15 minutes, then turn off the heat. Remove to a jar and let stand overnight in the fridge.

PIGS' EAR TERRINE

Preheat the oven to 325°F (163°C). Make sure the pigs' ears are free of all hair. If there is any visible hair, burn it off over an open flame. Toast the coriander seed and peppercorns in a dry pan over medium heat until they are fragrant. Add the toasted spices, stock, garlic, salt, and bay leaf to an oven-safe container that is small enough to fully submerge the ears in the stock. Cook for 3½ hours. You should be able to puncture the ears fully and easily with a fork. Remove the ears and save the liquid for other uses, like a stew or sauce. Line a terrine mold or loaf pan with parchment paper. Add the warm pigs' ears and cover with parchment. Press with a weight and refrigerate overnight.

TO ASSEMBLE

Thinly slice the pigs' ears and spoon the chili crisp on top, garnishing with micro cilantro.

SERVES 6 TO 8

MACROS PER SERVING

Net carbs: 0 grams
Protein: 11 grams
Fat: 60 grams
Calories: 584

PORK BELLY CONFIT

Almost any dish can be improved with a slice of nicely rendered pork belly. There are so many different techniques to turn this beautiful cut of meat into a shining star, and this one is up there as one of my favorites. Look for rendered pork fat (manteca) *in the Mexican aisle at the grocery store, but if it isn't available, just wrap up the pork belly loosely in tinfoil and it will confit itself. Check the Tip on page 95 for more information on how to safely cook with TCM no. 1 salt.*

- 3 tablespoons salt
- 2 tablespoons Swerve brown sugar
- 1 tablespoon ground black pepper
- 2 teaspoons ground fennel
- 2 teaspoons ground coriander
- 1 teaspoon TCM no. 1 salt
- 2 pounds (907 grams) pork belly
- 5 to 6 pounds (2.3 to 2.7 kilograms) pork fat

Mix salt, sugar, spices, and TCM and fully coat the pork belly. Let it cure in the fridge for 24 hours. Preheat the oven to 250°F (121°C). If the pork fat is in solid form, melt it in a large saucepan over low heat. Wash the cure off the pork belly, pat dry with paper towels, and submerge in pork fat in a roasting pan. Cover tightly with aluminum foil and cook for 6 hours. Remove from the fat and let cool, then wrap in plastic wrap and press with a large plate overnight in the fridge. When you're ready to use the pork belly, roast at 375°F (191°C) for 15 minutes uncovered, until crispy. Slice thinly.

DINNER

KALBI RIBS WITH SHIRATAKI NOODLE SALAD

I happened upon shirataki noodles while shopping for tofu in the vegan aisle at the grocery store. While they might not be quite as satisfying as traditional noodles, the texture is enjoyable, and they hold integrity with a variety of toppings. Here, thinly sliced short ribs are tenderized overnight and glazed with the marinating liquid. Grilling caramelizes the flavors onto the exterior of the meat, giving great depth to the dish. Amazuzuke, found in the same vegan section, is a Japanese pickle, which adds a crisp bite that is perfect with grilled meat.

SERVES 2

MACROS PER SERVING

Net carbs: 9 grams
Protein: 62 grams
Fat: 51 grams
Calories: 743

SHIRATAKI NOODLE SALAD

- 1 tablespoon sliced green onions
- 2 teaspoons mushroom soy sauce
- 2 teaspoons sesame oil
- 1 teaspoon oyster sauce
- ½ teaspoon minced ginger
- ¼ teaspoon chili flakes
- 1 (7-ounce [198-gram]) pack shirataki noodles
- 2 tablespoons canned sliced bamboo shoots
- 1 tablespoon roasted peanuts, crushed

TO ASSEMBLE

- 4 beef short ribs
- ½ cup (118 milliliters) chicken marinade (page 68)
- 1 cup (187 grams) shiratalki noodle salad
- ½ cup (68 grams) amazuzuke
- 4 tablespoons sambal (such as Huy Fong sambal oelek)
- Roasted peanuts, for garnish
- 2 tablespoons sesame oil
- Micro cilantro, for garnish

SHIRATAKI NOODLE SALAD

In a large bowl, mix the green onions, soy sauce, sesame oil, oyster sauce, ginger, and chili flakes. Toss with the shirataki noodles and bamboo shoots. Top with crushed roasted peanuts. Set aside.

TO ASSEMBLE

Marinate the short ribs in the chicken marinade overnight. Over a very hot grill, cook the short ribs, turning constantly, making sure not to burn too deeply, about 3 to 5 minutes per side. Once nicely charred, plate the ribs on top of the shirataki noodle salad and garnish with amazuzuke, sambal, peanuts, a drizzle of sesame oil, and micro cilantro.

BRAISED LAMB SHANK

Lamb comes in many forms, but none are as savory as a perfectly braised shank. Very few dishes are served on the bone, which either attracts you or makes you run for the hills. My carnivorous DNA is drawn to this dramatic bone-in preparation. Many people say they do not like lamb, but they just haven't tried the right lamb. The spice blend peppers the mouth, the jus sticks to the cheeks, and the meat evaporates with a graze of the tongue. This plate is a conversation stopper and a shirt destroyer.

SERVES 2

MACROS PER SERVING

Net carbs: 12 grams
Protein: 81 grams
Fat: 65 grams
Calories: 957

LAMB SHANK SPICE

2 tablespoons coriander seed
1 tablespoon fennel seed
1 tablespoon black peppercorns
2 teaspoons cumin seed
2 cardamom pods
2 tablespoons salt
1 tablespoon dried rosemary
1 tablespoon dried oregano
½ teaspoon ground cinnamon

TO ASSEMBLE

2 lamb shanks
6 tablespoons lamb shank spice
2 tablespoons olive oil
1 quart (946 milliliters) beef jus (page 29)
2 cups (473 milliliters) stock (page 64, or store-bought chicken or beef stock)
1 yellow onion, halved
8 whole cloves garlic
2 bunches small carrots, tops removed and reserved

LAMB SHANK SPICE

In a dry pan over medium heat, toast the coriander, fennel, peppercorns, cumin, and cardamom until fragrant. In a spice grinder or mortar and pestle, grind the toasted spices and then mix with the remaining ingredients until thoroughly blended.

TO ASSEMBLE

Cover the shanks with the spice blend and let sit, covered, in the fridge overnight. Preheat the oven to 425°F (218°C). Coat the shanks with the olive oil, place in a roasting pan, and roast for 45 minutes uncovered. In a medium saucepan over medium heat, warm the beef jus and stock together until simmering. Remove the shanks from the oven and decrease heat to 300°F (149°C). Pour the warm stock mixture into the lamb shank pan with the onions and garlic and cover the contents with aluminum foil. Cook for 2½ hours, add the carrots, and cook for another 45 minutes. Turn off the oven and let the shanks sit in the braise until desired tenderness is reached, about 1 hour. Strain the cooking liquid from the pan, add to a small saucepan, and cook over medium heat until reduced by half. Chop the reserved carrot tops, then use the sauce to coat the carrots and shanks and garnish with the tender carrot tops.

SERVES 2

MACROS PER SERVING

Net carbs: 5 grams
Protein: 10 grams
Fat: 43 grams
Calories: 527

ROASTED QUAIL

When you sit down to eat a meal you've prepared, you should be proud and excited to enjoy your creation. Having your own entire roasted bird can easily grant you those great feelings. Quail is surprisingly cost effective, yet rarely served in the home. I generally find them in the frozen section of the grocery store and defrost them in a brine the night before using. I enjoy roasting the romaine with the bird as it sops up all that caramelized roasted bird goodness. This chicken jus recipe goes with just about anything, so make sure to take note for next Thanksgiving.

CHICKEN JUS

- 1 pound (454 grams) roasted chicken scraps or bones
- 2 tablespoons olive oil
- 1 onion, roughly chopped
- 1 leek, roughly chopped
- 1 head garlic, broken into cloves
- 1½ tablespoons white peppercorns
- 1 teaspoon mustard seed
- ½ teaspoon black peppercorns
- Pinch of salt
- 1 quart (946 milliliters) keto white wine
- 1 gallon (3.8 liters) chicken stock
- 2 tablespoons fish sauce
- 1 tablespoon Worcestershire sauce
- ½ cup (118 milliliters) heavy cream
- 2 tablespoons Dijon mustard
- ¼ cup (57 grams) unsalted butter
- Lemon juice

ROASTED QUAIL

- 2 quail
- 2 tablespoons olive oil, divided
- 2 tablespoons salt, divided
- 4 cloves garlic
- 2 small heads romaine lettuce

TO ASSEMBLE

- 2 bunches enoki mushrooms
- 2 tablespoons olive oil
- Salt and pepper
- 6 tablespoons chicken jus, divided
- 2 roasted quail
- Micro mustard greens and marigold petals, for garnish

CHICKEN JUS

In a large pot over medium heat, sauté the roasted bones or scraps in olive oil until dark brown, about 5 to 10 minutes, then add in the onions, leeks, garlic, spices, and salt. Sauté on low until the onions are translucent, about 5 minutes, and then add the wine. Bring to medium heat and reduce until *au sec* (almost dry), 1 to 1½ hours, and then add in the chicken stock, fish sauce, and Worcestershire sauce. Bring to a vigorous simmer and reduce to a syrup consistency, about 2 hours. Add in the cream, Dijon mustard, and butter. Reduce again to achieve a syrup consistency and season with fresh lemon juice to taste. Strain, discard solids, and reserve jus.

ROASTED QUAIL

Preheat the oven to 350°F (177°C). Coat each quail in oil and season with salt inside and out. Add 2 cloves of garlic to each cavity and stuff each with a head of lettuce, leaving the ends protruding. Place each bird in a large cast-iron pan and roast for 45 minutes, turning the pan and basting after 20 minutes. Once the greens wilt, make sure to bend them into the cast-iron pan to soak up the drippings. Remove from the oven when a thermometer inserted into the thickest part of the breast or leg reads 165°F (74°C) and allow to rest while preparing the mushrooms.

TO ASSEMBLE

Break each enoki mushroom bunch in half and cut off the roots. Heat a large cast-iron pan over high heat until smoking hot and add the oil. Sear the mushrooms until golden brown, seasoning with salt and pepper in the pan. Add 3 tablespoons warm jus to the bottom of each plate and fan a cluster of the seared mushrooms on either side to create faux wings. Add the roasted quail on top with the wilted greens folded underneath to lift the bird up. Garnish with fresh greens and flower petals.

CORNISH GAME HENS WITH TRUFFLE JUS

Oven-roasted game hen is such a simple dish to make at home, and sometimes the classics shouldn't be messed with too much. I like to pair the hen with a very flavorful truffle jus, which lays a foundation of savoriness. Meanwhile, a fresh lemon emulsion dressing punctuates and cuts through the creamy sauce. I love little bundles of vegetables neatly tied together, but feel free to prepare this dish with a more rustic approach. Crispy basil adds a satisfying layer of herbaceousness.

SERVES 2

MACROS PER SERVING

Net carbs: 5 grams
Protein: 59 grams
Fat: 45 grams
Calories: 661

TRUFFLE JUS

1 cup (237 milliliters) chicken jus (page 115)
1 tablespoon truffle oil
½ teaspoon sherry vinegar
¼ teaspoon ground black pepper

LEMON EMULSION

¾ cup (177 milliliters) sunflower oil
¼ cup (59 milliliters) lemon juice
1 tablespoon Dijon mustard
1 teaspoon salt
⅛ teaspoon (½ of ¼ teaspoon) xanthan gum

CRISPY BASIL

Handful of basil leaves
Oil, for frying (such as canola, bran, or peanut oil)

TO ASSEMBLE

2 chives
2 bunches asparagus
2 teaspoons olive oil
Salt and pepper
2 Cornish game hens
4 tablespoons herbes de Provence
Crispy basil
2 black radishes, sliced mandoline thin
4 teaspoons lemon emulsion
4 tablespoons truffle jus, divided

TRUFFLE JUS

Combine all the ingredients in a small saucepan and warm over low heat. Remove from heat and set aside.

LEMON EMULSION

Blend all the ingredients together in a high-powered blender until fully emulsified and smooth. Set aside.

CRISPY BASIL

In a medium pan, heat about 2″ (5 cm) of oil to 325°F (163°C). Fry the basil for 10 to 20 seconds until bubbles stop forming and then drain on a paper towel.

TO ASSEMBLE

Bring a small saucepan of water to a boil, add the chives, blanch for 20 seconds, and then remove to an ice bath until ready to use. Preheat the oven to 425°F (218°C). Toss the asparagus with the olive oil, salt, and pepper, place in a roasting pan, and roast for 5 to 10 minutes, or until tender. Remove the asparagus from the pan and reduce the temperature to 375°F (191°C). Coat the birds with the herbes de Provence and salt and pepper inside and out and place in the roasting pan. Roast for 30 minutes until golden brown and the internal temperature reaches 165°F (74°C), then turn off the oven. In a small saucepan, warm the truffle jus. Tie the roasted asparagus into a bunch using a blanched chive. Toss the crispy basil and radishes with the lemon emulsion. Spread the truffle jus on 2 plates and top with the hens and the vegetables.

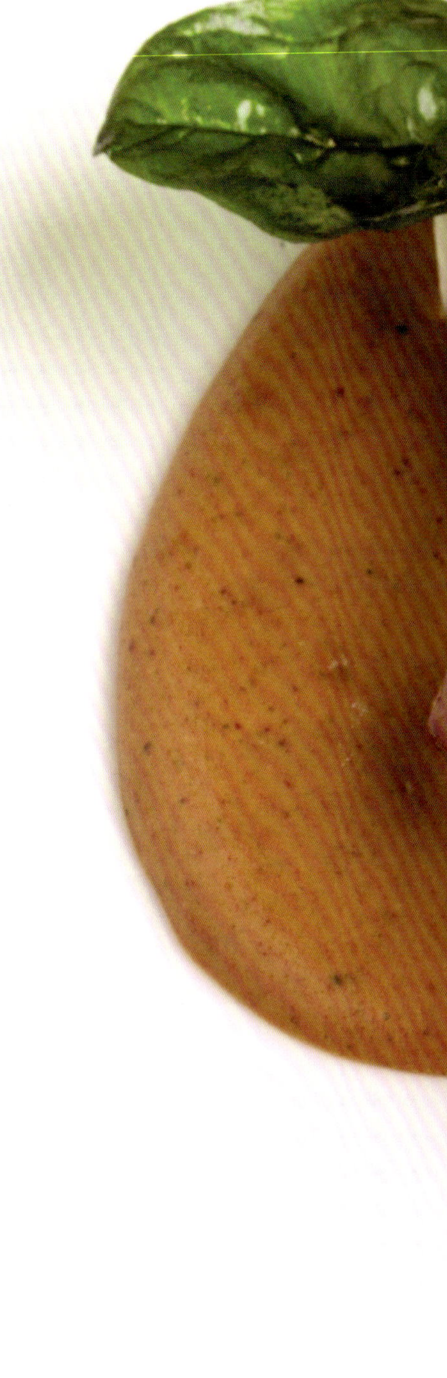

SERVES 2

MACROS PER SERVING

Net carbs: 8 grams
Protein: 18 grams
Fat: 17 grams
Calories: 261

GRILLED CHICKEN AND ALI'I

We originally cooked this chicken over a binchotan grill with Japanese charcoal on the beach in Lahaina on the west coast of Maui. Ali'i is Hawaiian for "royalty," and these mushrooms are commonly known as king trumpets and are a favorite here in the islands. I named my local business Ali'i Chefs and Catering after them as they are one of my favorite ingredients. The marinade is best done 24 hours in advance to let all the flavors penetrate the meat. Cooking over an open fire is always preferred, but if that isn't an option, consider investing in a well-seasoned cast-iron skillet. Just make sure your windows are open when it smokes up!

NAMASU

1 cucumber, sliced mandoline thin
1 tablespoon salt
1 tablespoon light soy sauce
2 teaspoons lemon juice

PARSLEY OIL

2 bunches parsley
1 cup (237 milliliters) olive oil

SPICY CHICKEN MARINADE

½ cup (118 milliliters) sriracha
2 tablespoons soy sauce
2 tablespoons chopped garlic
2 tablespoons sambal (such as Huy Fong sambal oelek)
2 tablespoons Swerve brown sugar
1 tablespoon sesame oil
1 tablespoon chicken bouillon powder
4 teaspoons red wine vinegar
2 teaspoons salt

TO ASSEMBLE

2 boneless, skinless chicken thighs
Spicy chicken marinade
4 king trumpet mushrooms (ali'i)
4 tablespoons shaved radish
1 bunch watercress
2 tablespoons parsley oil
½ cup (80 grams) namasu
2 lime wedges

NAMASU

Toss the cucumber with the salt and let sit for 1 hour. Wash with ice-cold water and strain with cheesecloth. Toss with the light soy sauce and lemon juice and set aside.

PARSLEY OIL

Blend the parsley and oil together in a high-powered blender for 8 minutes. Strain through cheesecloth and discard solids. Set aside.

SPICY CHICKEN MARINADE

In a small bowl, using a whisk or a fork, blend all the ingredients together into a paste.

TO ASSEMBLE

Coat the chicken thighs with ½ cup (118 milliliters) of the marinade and marinate in the fridge overnight. When ready to cook, bring a charcoal grill to high heat. Sear the mushrooms and grill the chicken, turning frequently, about 4 to 5 minutes per side, glazing the chicken with the remaining marinade as it cooks, until nicely charred and the internal temperature of the chicken reaches 165°F (74°C). Toss the radish and watercress in the parsley oil and serve alongside the chicken, ali'i, namasu, and lime wedges.

SERVES 2

MACROS PER SERVING

Net carbs: 9 grams
Protein: 21 grams
Fat: 19 grams
Calories: 291

CRISPY DUCK WITH CARROT PUREE AND BLACKBERRY JUS

In my opinion, people should eat duck more often. Perhaps the cooking process is seen as intimidating, and that's what scares folks away. For me, duck is best prepared in three major ways: Peking style (a Beijing specialty), confit (the easiest but most time-consuming method), and seared medium-rare with crispy skin. Starting with a cold pan and scoring the skin helps render the fat to achieve perfectly crispy skin while pan-searing.

BLACKBERRY JUS

1 cup (237 milliliters) chicken jus (page 115)
1 tablespoon red wine vinegar
8 blackberries, halved
Salt

CARROT PUREE

2 carrots, peeled and diced large
1 tablespoon olive oil
Salt and pepper
5 cloves garlic, chopped
2 shallots, julienned
½ cup (118 milliliters) keto white wine
½ cup (118 milliliters) heavy cream
¼ cup (57 grams) unsalted butter, softened
1 teaspoon lemon zest
1 teaspoon lemon juice

CRISPY SHISO

1 bunch shiso leaves
Oil, for frying (such as canola, bran, or peanut oil)

TO ASSEMBLE

½ cup (41 grams) chopped eggplant
2 tablespoons olive oil
Salt and pepper
2 duck breasts
½ cup (123 grams) carrot puree
4 crispy shiso leaves
4 French breakfast radishes, sliced thin
Heirloom arugula, for garnish
½ cup (118 milliliters) blackberry jus

BLACKBERRY JUS

In a small saucepan over medium heat, simmer the chicken jus, vinegar, and blackberries together just until warmed, gently crushing the blackberries to release the juices. Season with salt and set aside.

CARROT PUREE

In a large pan over medium heat, sauté the carrots with the olive oil, season with salt and pepper to taste, and cook until softened, about 4 to 5 minutes. Add the garlic and shallots and sweat down with the carrots until the shallots are translucent, 1 to 2 minutes. Add the wine and reduce until almost dry. Add the cream and cook over low heat until the carrots easily fall apart. Remove from the heat and blend in a high-powered blender with the butter, lemon zest, and lemon juice. Season with salt and pepper.

CRISPY SHISO

Heat a deep fryer or a large pot of oil over medium-high heat to 350°F (177°C) and drop in the shiso leaves one at a time, giving them space to expand. Fry for 20 to 30 seconds and drain on a paper towel.

TO ASSEMBLE

Preheat the oven to 425°F (218°C) and toss the eggplant with the olive oil, salt, and pepper, spread onto a baking sheet, and roast for 10 minutes, or until lightly browned. Set aside. Score the duck breasts in a crisscross pattern. Add the duck to a cold large pan, skin side down, and heat over low heat, rendering out the fat by pressing with medium pressure on the bird as it cooks. After 5 minutes, increase the temperature to medium and pour out the fat that is being rendered, saving it for another use. Once the skin is crispy, flip and sear the other side of the duck for about 20 seconds until just seared. Remove from the heat and let rest for 10 minutes. Slice and serve atop the carrot puree, garnish with the crispy shiso, sliced radishes, and arugula, and drizzle with the blackberry jus.

RADISH SCALE SALMON WITH CHIPOTLE DASHI

This dish was so much fun to make! While I know many people at home would like to eat their food within an hour and without pulling all their hair out in the process, I wanted to showcase the planking scale method for the overachievers of the world. This dish highlights multiple foundational techniques, including making a proper dashi, which requires using quality ingredients and respecting the delicate process. This dish will taste great with or without a meticulous organizing of radish puzzle pieces, but if you have the time, this technique is a showstopper.

SERVES 2

MACROS PER SERVING

Net carbs: 8 grams
Protein: 25 grams
Fat: 48 grams
Calories: 564

COURT BOUILLON

2 quarts (1.9 liters) water
1 cup (130 grams) julienned onion
1 cup (122 grams) sliced carrot
5 cloves garlic, sliced
1 lemon, halved
1 tablespoon coriander seed
1 tablespoon black peppercorns
1 tablespoon fish sauce
1 tablespoon salt
½ teaspoon chili flakes

CHIPOTLE DASHI

4 ounces (113 grams) kombu
2 dried chipotle peppers
1 quart (946 milliliters) cold water
4 ounces (113 grams) katsuobushi (bonito flakes)
1 clove garlic
1 tablespoon fish sauce
1 teaspoon salt

RADISH SCALES

⅓ cup (76 grams) unsalted butter
20 slices radish, cut on a mandoline
20 slices turnip, cut on a mandoline

TO ASSEMBLE

8 baby zucchini, sliced in half lengthwise
¼ cup (59 milliliters) olive oil
Salt and pepper
1 quart (946 milliliters) court bouillon
2 (4-ounce [113-gram]) salmon fillets
Radish scales
2 cups (473 milliliters) chipotle dashi
2 tablespoons ogo seaweed
Pea tendrils, for garnish

COURT BOUILLON

In a large pot over medium heat, bring all the ingredients to a simmer and cook for 30 minutes. Turn off the heat and let stand for another 30 minutes. Strain out the solids and reserve the bouillon.

CHIPOTLE DASHI

Combine the kombu and chipotle peppers with the cold water in a large saucepan and bring to a simmer slowly over medium-low. It should take up to 30 minutes. Turn off the heat, add the remaining ingredients, and let sit for 30 minutes. Strain through a fine-mesh strainer.

RADISH SCALES

Cut out two 4″ x 4″ (10 x 10 cm) pieces of parchment and spread each evenly with the butter. Refrigerate for 20 minutes. Stamp out the radish and turnip slices with a mold to make equal round pieces. Carefully lay out the radish and turnip pieces, alternating vegetables, over the butter-topped parchment. For each row, alternate with the colors above it. Once all the butter is covered, refrigerate. Remove from the fridge and allow to come to room temperature 15 minutes before using.

TO ASSEMBLE

Preheat the oven to 425°F (218°C). Toss the zucchini in the olive oil and season with salt and pepper. In a roasting pan, roast for 10 minutes, or until tender. Meanwhile, in a large pot, bring the court bouillon to a simmer and poach the salmon until about 50 percent cooked through, 4 to 5 minutes. Pat dry with a towel and let sit for 5 minutes. Lay one of the parchments of radish scales on top of each fillet and cut out the shape of the pieces of fish so they perfectly match up. Place the fillets in a steamer basket or bamboo steamer and steam for 3 minutes, then carefully remove the parchment. Warm the dashi and divide between 2 bowls, layer in the roasted zucchini, and add the fish in the center. Garnish with the ogo seaweed and pea tendrils.

YELLOW PORK CURRY WITH WILD MUSTARD GREENS

Curry is a broad genre of food that can mean many different combinations of spices, ingredients, and styles depending on where it's being served. The name curry *was originally applied to all sauce-based dishes from India. In America we really don't have any genre of food as varied as curry because the origins of Indian curry date back to 2600 BCE. Very few foods have diversified into so many subgenres, and this variation is just a hodgepodge of what I wanted to eat that day. I am in awe of the diversity of ingredients and flavors that curry can encompass, and it would take a lifetime to truly experience all the variations of this international cuisine.*

SERVES 2

MACROS PER SERVING

Net carbs: 8 grams
Protein: 40 grams
Fat: 47 grams
Calories: 615

CILANTRO OIL

- 2 cups (473 milliliters) canola oil
- 2 bunches cilantro
- 2 bunches chives

YELLOW PORK CURRY

- 2 tablespoons canola oil
- 1 pound (454 grams) pork butt, cut into 1″ (2.5 cm) chunks
- ¼ cup (43 grams) sliced bell peppers
- ½ cup (35 grams) quartered cremini mushrooms
- 2 tablespoons yellow curry paste
- 1 tablespoon minced garlic
- 1 (13.5-ounce [400 milliliters]) can full-fat coconut milk
- 1 cup (237 milliliters) chicken stock
- 1 teaspoon fish sauce

TO ASSEMBLE

- 2 cups (473 milliliters) yellow pork curry
- 2 tablespoons cilantro oil
- 2 teaspoons lime zest
- Watercress and wild mustard greens, for garnish

CILANTRO OIL

Blend the oil, cilantro, and chives in a high-powered blender for 5 minutes. Pass through a fine-mesh strainer or cheesecloth. Set aside.

YELLOW PORK CURRY

Heat a large pan over medium-high heat until hot, add the oil, and sear the pork, peppers, and mushrooms until browned on all sides, about 4 minutes. Add the curry paste and garlic and stir to coat. Add the coconut milk, stock, and fish sauce. Bring to a low simmer and cook for 1 hour over low heat until the pork is tender and cooked through.

TO ASSEMBLE

Add 1 cup (237 ml) curry to each bowl and garnish with cilantro oil, lime zest, watercress, and mustard greens.

LAMB CHOPS WITH PARSLEY PANADE AND CREAMED CHARD

After experimenting for a while, I knew I wanted to introduce a panade, a paste traditionally made with milk and bread, to one of my grilled dishes. Lamb begs for herbs, which is why I chose to incorporate that element in the preparation. Rainbow chard can just as easily be sautéed with garlic and lemon juice and substituted in this dish, but there's something about having a creamed green with roasted meat that I love. It gives me a certain steak-house satisfaction without having to break the bank or get tempted by a loaded baked potato staring me in the face. I enjoy broccoli steamed with salt and a touch of extra-virgin olive oil, but the foamy cream is a fun way to have the kids enjoy getting their vitamins.

SERVES 2

MACROS PER SERVING

Net carbs: 12 grams
Protein: 18 grams
Fat: 42 grams
Calories: 498

BROCCOLI CREAM

1 bunch broccoli, stalks removed
½ cup (118 milliliters) whole milk
¼ cup (59 milliliters) heavy cream
1 tablespoon soy lecithin
1 clove garlic
1 teaspoon salt

CREAMED CHARD

3 cloves garlic, sliced thin
1 tablespoon brunoise-cut shallots
1 tablespoon olive oil
1 bunch chard
½ cup (118 milliliters) heavy cream
2 tablespoons sour cream
1 teaspoon lemon juice
Salt and pepper

PARSLEY PANADE

Oil, for frying (such as canola, bran, or peanut oil)
Leaves from 1 bunch parsley
½ cup (48 grams) almond flour
1 teaspoon salt
1 egg white

ROASTED CARROTS

1 bunch small carrots, peeled, trimmed, and cut into quarters
1 tablespoon olive oil
Salt and pepper

LAMB CHOPS

1 rack lamb chops
Salt and pepper
4 tablespoons parsley panade

TO ASSEMBLE

1 cup creamed chard
4 roasted carrots
8 ribs lamb chops
4 tablespoons broccoli cream
Micro lemon balm, for garnish

BROCCOLI CREAM

Steam the broccoli for 10 minutes until very soft. In a small saucepan over medium heat, bring the remaining ingredients to a simmer. Blend with the cooked broccoli in a high-powered blender until smooth. Before using, blend again with an immersion blender to create a top layer of foamy goodness. Scoop the foam off the top. Save the liquid for another use.

CREAMED CHARD

In a large pan over medium heat, sauté the garlic and shallots in the oil for 1 minute. Add the chard and sauté until wilted. Add the cream and sour cream, stir to combine, and then cook over medium heat until thickened, about 2 minutes. Season with the lemon juice, salt, and pepper.

PARSLEY PANADE

In a medium pan, heat about 2″ (5 cm) of oil over high heat until shimmering. Fry the parsley leaves until fully cooked and crispy and bubbles stop forming. Remove, drain, and then blend with the remaining ingredients in a food processor until well combined. Let chill for 1 hour before using.

ROASTED CARROTS

Preheat the oven to 400°F (204°C). Put a baking sheet in the oven and let it warm up for 10 minutes. Meanwhile, toss the carrots with the oil, salt, and pepper. Add the carrots to the scorching baking sheet and return to the oven, roasting for 10 minutes until just tender. Remove from the oven and let cool.

LAMB CHOPS

Reduce the oven temperature to 350°F (177°C). Season the lamb rack with salt and pepper. Heat a large cast-iron skillet over medium-high heat until quite hot, then sear the rack on all sides. Remove to a paper-towel-lined plate and let rest for 10 minutes. Coat the rack with a thin layer of the panade, place in a roasting pan, and roast, uncovered, until an internal temperature of 145°F (63°C) is reached, about 4 to 5 minutes per side. Let rest and slice into double rack portions.

TO ASSEMBLE

Divide the creamed chard and roasted carrots onto 2 plates. Layer 4 ribs of lamb chops atop each plate. Add the broccoli cream and garnish with the micro lemon balm.

SERVES 2

MACROS PER SERVING

Net carbs: 8 grams
Protein: 41 grams
Fat: 39 grams
Calories: 447

FILET MIGNON WITH CAULIFLOWER FOAM AND CARROT BASKET

Steak is always a pleasure to eat, but I believe it should be enjoyed as a special occasion. Filet mignon is a great cut of meat due to its low fat content and tenderness, so you can bolster up the fat in the accoutrements. The cauliflower foam is denser than it may appear, and a light hand on the iSi dispenser is needed (I painted the plate and my pants on the first attempt). The carrot basket is a fun garnish that can be added to just about any dish to introduce some crispy deliciousness.

CARROT BASKET

1 cup (110 grams) spiralized carrots, divided
Oil, for frying (such as canola, bran, or peanut oil)
Salt

CAULIFLOWER FOAM

1 cup (107 grams) chopped cauliflower
½ cup (118 milliliters) heavy cream
¼ cup (59 milliliters) whole milk
2 tablespoons shredded white cheddar cheese
1 tablespoon soy lecithin
1 teaspoon salt

TO ASSEMBLE

2 (4-ounce [113-gram]) filets mignons
Salt and pepper
½ cup (35 grams) maitake mushrooms
½ cup (30 grams) cauliflower foam
2 carrot baskets
Baby kale, for garnish
¼ cup (59 milliliters) beef jus (page 29)

CARROT BASKET

In a mesh pasta basket, in a deep fryer with oil heated to 300°F (149°C), fry ¼ cup (28 grams) of the spiralized carrots at a time. Shake the basket continually while frying to gently make a ball form. Keep cooking and shaking until fully cooked and crisp, about 1 minute. Remove to a paper-towel-lined plate and season with salt.

CAULIFLOWER FOAM

Place the cauliflower in a steamer basket or bamboo steamer and steam until it is very soft, about 20 minutes. In a medium saucepan over medium heat, combine the cauliflower with the remaining ingredients and bring to a simmer, cooking for 15 minutes. Add to a high-powered blender and blend until smooth. Strain with a fine-mesh strainer, discard the solids, allow the liquid to cool, and charge in an iSi container with 2 nitrous cartridges.

TO ASSEMBLE

Season the steak heavily with salt and pepper, then grill over an open flame or on a gas grill on high heat until browned on all sides, about 4 minutes per side for medium-rare. Rest for 10 minutes and then slice. Sear the maitake over high heat and season with salt and pepper. Pipe the cauliflower foam onto 2 plates, then layer with the sliced steak, seared mushrooms, carrot baskets, and baby kale. Drizzle with the beef jus.

SERVES 2

MACROS PER SERVING

Net carbs: 9 grams
Protein: 39 grams
Fat: 56 grams
Calories: 696

PINE NUT–ENCRUSTED MAHI MAHI

Choucroute is an Alsatian dish typically enjoyed with sausages or big double bone-in pork chops, but I love to add it to everything. It's really just a sped-up warm sauerkraut that can bring balance to most of the food involved in a keto diet. Any cabbage can be used, but I was lucky to have beautiful Chinese red cabbage available at the farm during this shoot. I like to keep a jar of choucroute in the fridge for at least a month before using it, but it is ready to use in as little as three days. The pine nuts do not necessarily need to be encrusted on the dish, but I just love the presentation. For the pesto, I like to keep it broken to show off all the herbaceous chlorophyll. Mahi mahi is a Hawaiian favorite and widely known as dorado on the mainland.

THAI BASIL PESTO

- 2 bunches Thai basil leaves, chopped
- 1 bunch mint leaves, chopped
- 1 bunch parsley leaves, chopped
- 1 cup (237 milliliters) olive oil
- 4 tablespoons almonds
- 1 tablespoon minced garlic
- 1 teaspoon lemon zest
- 2 cups (160 grams) microplaned Parmesan
- 2 teaspoons chili flakes
- 1 teaspoon lemon juice
- Salt and white pepper

RED CABBAGE CHOUCROUTE

- 1 head Chinese red cabbage (red Napa cabbage)
- 2 tablespoons salt, divided
- ¼ cup (59 milliliters) red wine vinegar
- 1 teaspoon caraway seed
- 2 cloves garlic
- 2 tablespoons water
- 1 tablespoon Swerve sugar

TO ASSEMBLE

- 2 (6-ounce [170-gram]) fillets mahi mahi
- 2 tablespoons salt
- 2 tablespoons canola oil
- 4 tablespoons aioli
- 6 tablespoons pine nuts
- 6 tablespoons Thai basil pesto
- 1 cup (240 grams) red cabbage choucroute
- Nasturtiums, zucchini flowers, and micro dill, for garnish

THAI BASIL PESTO

Bring a large pot of water to boil and blanch the Thai basil for 20 seconds, then plunge into an ice bath. In a high-powered blender, combine the Thai basil with the mint, parsley, oil, almonds, garlic, and lemon zest and blend until smooth. Add the cheese, chili flakes, and lemon juice and blend again. Add a touch of water if needed to reach desired consistency. Season with salt and white pepper.

RED CABBAGE CHOUCROUTE

Chiffonade the cabbage and mix in 1 tablespoon of the salt. Let stand in the fridge, uncovered, for 1 hour and drain, then add to a large bowl. In a small saucepan over medium-low heat, warm the red wine vinegar with the caraway, garlic, water, sugar, and the remaining 1 tablespoon of salt. Pour over the cabbage and let stand, covered, for at least 12 hours, but preferably for 3 full days. Drain and wring out the excess pickling liquid before use.

TO ASSEMBLE

Rub the mahi mahi with salt and cure in the fridge for 2 hours. Preheat the oven to 350°F (177°C). Wash the salt from the fish and pat dry with paper towels. Add the oil to a large pan over medium-high heat and sear one side of the fish for about 3 minutes, keeping the center raw. Remove from the pan and place onto a baking sheet seared side up. Spread 2 tablespoons of the aioli on top of each fillet. Add the pine nuts to coat. Roast for 15 minutes, or until fully cooked. Smear each plate with 3 tablespoons of the pesto and top each with ½ cup (120 grams) of the choucroute. Layer the fish atop the choucroute and garnish with nasturtiums, zucchini flowers, and micro dill.

COD À LA MEUNIÈRE

Meunière, also known as the miller's way, is a traditional and simple dish from France in which fish is generally floured and then cooked with brown butter. This rendition skips the flour. Keith couldn't get over this dish when he tried it after shooting. It was his absolute favorite. Some of the best keto dishes are simple renditions of classics. Brown butter seasoned with fresh lemon juice and capers will never go out of style.

SERVES 1

MACROS PER SERVING

Net carbs: 9 grams
Protein: 33 grams
Fat: 74 grams
Calories: 834

6 ounces (170 grams) cod
Salt and pepper
2 tablespoons olive oil
¼ cup (57 grams) unsalted butter
3 tablespoons capers, rinsed and drained
3 tablespoons microplaned garlic
1 tablespoon lemon juice
2 tablespoons minced chives

Season the fish with salt and pepper and let stand for 20 minutes. In a medium pan, heat the oil over high heat and once it starts smoking, add the fish and turn down the temperature to medium. Sear both sides of the fish for about 2 minutes per side until just cooked through and remove from the pan. Turn the heat down to low and add the butter, capers, and garlic. Sauté for 3 to 5 minutes, or until the butter begins to brown. Add the lemon juice, remove from the heat, and pour over the fish. Top with the chives.

DESSERT

SERVES 3

MACROS PER SERVING

Net carbs: 12 grams
Protein: 12 grams
Fat: 35 grams
Calories: 411

PEPPERED STRAWBERRY SHORTCAKE

Some may think this dish is blasphemous, some may call me crazy, and some may revolt at the idea of putting chili flakes with strawberries. This dish can easily be tweaked to satiate a normal person's cravings, but if this plate excites you, don't let convention get in your way. One of the toughest parts of keto is building textures, as carbohydrates contribute much to the world of crunch. Isomalt glass is a fun confection that has zero calories and can give some next-level crunch to any dessert. You may have to order isomalt online, but it can be found at many local bake shops. I enjoy giving my palate surprises, and this dish brings the heat. If you want to keep it traditional, be my guest, but the safest route doesn't always bring the best rewards.

POACHED STRAWBERRIES

- 1 cup (152 grams) halved strawberries
- 4 tablespoons sugar-free strawberry jam
- 1 tablespoon Swerve granular sugar
- 1 tablespoon keto white wine
- 1 teaspoon lemon juice
- 1 teaspoon lemon zest
- Pinch of salt
- Pinch of chili flakes

SHORTCAKE

- 2½ cups (241 grams) almond flour
- ½ cup (60 grams) coconut flour
- ¼ cup (48 grams) Swerve granular sugar
- ½ teaspoon baking soda
- ½ teaspoon salt
- ½ cup (118 milliliters) coconut milk
- ¼ cup (30 grams) sour cream
- ½ teaspoon lemon juice
- ½ teaspoon lemon zest

STABILIZED FIVE-SPICE CREAM

- 3 tablespoons water
- 1 teaspoon unflavored gelatin
- 1 cup (237 milliliters) heavy cream
- 2 tablespoons Swerve confectioners' sugar
- 2 teaspoons five-spice powder
- ¼ teaspoon vanilla extract

STRAWBERRY ISOMALT GLASS

- ½ cup (125 grams) isomalt
- 2 tablespoons water
- 4 drops red food dye
- 4 drops yellow food dye
- 3 drops food-grade strawberry essential oil

TO ASSEMBLE

- 1 cup (152 grams) poached strawberries
- 6 squares shortcake
- ¾ cup (177 milliliters) stabilized five-spice cream
- 9 pieces strawberry isomalt glass
- ¾ teaspoon chili flakes

POACHED STRAWBERRIES

In a small saucepan over medium-low heat, simmer all the ingredients for 10 minutes until reduced and syrupy. Set aside.

SHORTCAKE

Preheat the oven to 350°F (177°C) and grease a 6″ x 6″ (15 x 15 cm) pan. In a large bowl, mix the almond flour, coconut flour, sugar, baking soda, and salt together. In a medium bowl, combine the coconut milk, sour cream, lemon juice, and lemon zest. Add the wet to the dry ingredients and mix until the batter just comes together. Pour into the prepared pan and bake for 20 minutes, or until golden brown. Let cool on the counter, then slice into 2″ x 2″ (5 x 5 cm) squares.

STABILIZED FIVE-SPICE CREAM

In a small bowl, add the water to the gelatin and let bloom for 10 minutes. Add the hydrated gelatin to a small sauté pan and cook on low until viscous, about 5 minutes. Remove from the heat, pour back into the bowl, and let cool to room temperature. In a large bowl with an electric mixer, whisk the cream, confectioners' sugar, five-spice, and vanilla until stiff peaks form. Add the cooled gelatin and whisk until fully combined. Transfer to a pastry bag and store in the fridge until ready to use.

STRAWBERRY ISOMALT GLASS

Line a baking sheet with parchment paper. In a small saucepan, bring the isomalt and water to a boil without mixing it. Bring the mixture up to 320°F (160°C), using a candy thermometer to measure. Be careful not to go above this temperature. Remove from the heat and very carefully add the food dye and essential oil. Mix in waves with a toothpick to make streaks. Carefully pour it onto the parchment paper and spread out using an offset spatula. When it begins to cool, in 1 to 2 minutes, mold the isomalt to whatever shape you desire.

TO ASSEMBLE

Warm the poached strawberries and place ⅓ cup (51 grams) on the bottom of each plate. Top with a square of shortcake. Pipe about 2 tablespoons of the stabilized cream on top of each shortcake, top with another square of shortcake, and pipe on more cream. Garnish with pieces of strawberry isomalt glass and ¼ teaspoon of chili flakes on each.

PEANUT BUTTER EGG

In traditional fine dining, the eggshell is a cool vessel used to serve an appetizer or intermezzo, perhaps with heaping spoonfuls of caviar and a light frothy concoction to titillate the appetite. I thought it would be fun to close dinner in this fashion. You eat with your eyes first, and this dish will definitely leave an impression on your friends and family. Pot de crème is an easy win as a dessert and perfectly holds its quality in the fridge for a week. You can find tools online to help remove the top of an egg, as well as food-grade sanitizer that can be used to prepare the shell for serving. Of course, any small and fancy vessel would work just fine if you don't want to fight with an eggshell, but the unexpected and refined presentation is a treat in itself.

SERVES 2

MACROS PER SERVING

Net carbs: 11 grams
Protein: 18 grams
Fat: 42 grams
Calories: 494

PEANUT BUTTER POT DE CRÈME

- ¼ cup (48 grams) Swerve sugar
- 5 egg yolks
- 2 cups (473 milliliters) heavy cream
- ½ cup (118 milliliters) whole milk
- ½ cup (129 grams) unsweetened smooth peanut butter

WHITE CHOCOLATE CHANTILLY

- ¼ cup (40 grams) Lily's white chocolate chips
- 2 cups (473 milliliters) heavy cream
- ¼ cup (48 grams) Swerve sugar
- Pinch of salt

TO ASSEMBLE

- 4 tablespoons peanut butter pot de crème
- 2 eggshells, tops removed, emptied, and sanitized (see headnote)
- 2 tablespoons white chocolate Chantilly
- 1 tablespoon roasted peanuts

PEANUT BUTTER POT DE CRÈME

In a medium bowl, whisk the sugar and egg yolks together. In a medium saucepan over medium-low heat, bring the cream, milk, and peanut butter to a simmer, stirring constantly. Slowly pour half of the peanut butter mixture into the egg yolks, whisking constantly. Add another half while whisking. Return the mixture to the saucepan, whisk to blend, and cook over low heat for 2 to 3 minutes until thickened. Transfer to a piping bag and let sit overnight in the fridge to solidify.

WHITE CHOCOLATE CHANTILLY

In a double boiler over medium heat, melt the chocolate. In a medium bowl with an electric mixer, whip the remaining ingredients together until stiff peaks form, then slowly add the white chocolate while mixing. Transfer to a piping bag.

TO ASSEMBLE

Pipe the peanut butter pot de crème into the clean empty eggshells. Pipe on the white chocolate Chantilly and garnish with roasted peanuts.

MINT ICE CREAM WITH ALMOND MADELEINES

Supermarket keto ice cream is gross. There, I've said it. I've tried tons of different brands and none of them give me an ounce of satisfaction. The solution is to make your own ice cream at home. This is actually a plausible feat because you don't need an ice cream maker to do it. Some planning ahead will be in order, but the reward is sweet . . . wink-wink. The magic chocolate shell is such a simple addition that gives a wonderful crunch and makes the dish memorable. Feel free to temper the chocolate in a microwave. The only problem with this recipe is stopping at two madeleines.

SERVES 2

MACROS PER SERVING

Net carbs: 6 grams
Protein: 8 grams
Fat: 56 grams
Calories: 560

ALMOND MADELEINES

- 2 tablespoons unsalted butter, melted (for greasing pan)
- ½ cup (96 grams) Swerve granular sugar
- ¼ cup (57 grams) unsalted butter, softened
- 2 cups (193 grams) almond flour
- 2 tablespoons Swerve confectioners' sugar
- 2 tablespoons finely chopped almonds
- ½ teaspoon salt
- ½ teaspoon cinnamon

MAGIC CHOCOLATE SHELL

- 2 cups (480 grams) Lily's dark chocolate chips
- ⅔ cup (145 grams) coconut oil
- Pinch of salt

MINT ICE CREAM

- 1 (13.5-ounce [400 milliliters]) can full-fat coconut milk
- ½ ripe avocado
- 4 tablespoons allulose
- 1 teaspoon vanilla extract
- 4 drops peppermint extract
- 2 drops green food dye
- Pinch of salt
- ½ cup (118 milliliters) heavy cream, whipped

TO ASSEMBLE

- 4 tablespoons magic chocolate shell mixture
- 2 cups (267 grams) mint ice cream
- 2 tablespoons chopped almonds
- 4 almond madeleines
- Marigold flower heads, for garnish

ALMOND MADELEINES

Preheat the oven to 350°F (177°C). Grease a madeleine pan with the melted butter and put in the freezer for 30 minutes. In a large bowl with an electric mixer, cream the granular sugar and butter together until fluffy, about 3 to 4 minutes, then beat in the remaining ingredients. Add dollops of dough to the prepared madeleine pan. Bake for 15 minutes, or until golden brown. Let cool on a wire rack.

MAGIC CHOCOLATE SHELL

In a double boiler over medium-low heat, warm the ingredients together until smooth. Remove from the heat and dip the cooled madeleines into the chocolate shell, then transfer to a parchment-lined plate and place in the freezer until the chocolate is set. Set aside the double boiler with the remaining chocolate shell mixture in it.

MINT ICE CREAM

Blend the coconut milk, avocado, allulose, vanilla, peppermint, food dye, and salt until smooth. Lightly fold in the whipped cream. Freeze the mixture for 1 to 3 hours until firmed up and use immediately. If you've made it well in advance, it will need to thaw until scoopable as it gets very hard over time.

TO ASSEMBLE

Chill 2 bowls in the freezer until cold. In the double boiler, rewarm the chocolate shell mixture. Pipe or scoop 1 cup (134 grams) of ice cream into each chilled bowl and gently pour 2 tablespoons of the warm chocolate shell mixture on top of each. Quickly add 1 tablespoon of chopped almonds to each before the shell hardens. Serve with 2 madeleines each and marigold flower heads for the razzle-dazzle.

MAKES 10 CAKES

MACROS PER SERVING

Net carbs: 3 grams
Protein: 11 grams
Fat: 72 grams
Calories: 704

FLOURLESS CHOCOLATE CAKE

This dish is the chocolate bomb that will calm your cravings and defy the standards of losing weight. Crémeaux *translates to "creamy" in French and is essentially a crème anglaise emulsified with chocolate. The process of whisking the egg yolks and sugar will give the mixture a flawlessly creamy texture. I love pairing my chocolate with a side of chocolate.*

CHOCOLATE CRÉMEAUX

4 egg yolks
¼ cup (48 grams) Swerve sugar
1½ cups (355 milliliters) heavy cream
1 cup (240 grams) Lily's dark chocolate chips
½ cup (118 milliliters) whole milk
¼ teaspoon salt

FLOURLESS CHOCOLATE CAKE

8 eggs
¼ cup (48 grams) allulose
1 pound (454 grams) Lily's dark baking chocolate
2 cups (454 grams) unsalted butter, softened

TO ASSEMBLE

½ cup (84 grams) Lily's milk chocolate chips
1 tablespoon heavy cream
½ teaspoon salt
10 flourless chocolate cakes
Chocolate crémeaux

CHOCOLATE CRÉMEAUX

In a medium bowl, whisk the egg yolks and sugar together. In a medium saucepan over medium-low heat, bring the remaining ingredients to a simmer. One tablespoon at a time, add the hot cream mixture into the yolk mixture, whisking constantly. Once combined, return the mixture to the saucepan and simmer over low heat for 2 minutes, whisking constantly, until thickened but not curdled. Remove from the heat and pass through a fine-mesh strainer. Let cool slightly, then press plastic wrap on the top of the crémeaux to prevent a skin from forming. Refrigerate overnight to set.

FLOURLESS CHOCOLATE CAKE

Preheat the oven to 325°F (163°C). In a stand mixer, beat the eggs and allulose for about 5 minutes until doubled in size. Melt the dark chocolate and butter together in a double boiler over medium-low and remove to a medium bowl, letting it sit for 10 to 15 minutes until cooled but still slightly warm. Fold the egg mixture into the chocolate mixture one-third at a time until fully incorporated. Pipe into ten 4-ounce (118-milliliter) molds and bake for 20 minutes, or until risen and firm. Let cool completely and then remove from the molds and place the individual cakes on plates to serve.

TO ASSEMBLE

In a double boiler, combine the milk chocolate chips, cream, and salt and heat over medium-low until fully melted. Drizzle about two-thirds of the chocolate over the top of the cakes to give an outer glaze. Top each cake with a quenelle (an elegant spoonful) of crémeaux and drizzle again with the chocolate mixture.

CHOCOLATE CAKE WITH SMOKED-MILK PANNA COTTA

Lily's chocolate is incredible. I like to use it to balance out recipes even when I am not on keto. The great thing about it is that you don't have to feel guilty eating a handful while preparing a dish or to satisfy a late-night craving. This dish is a double whammy as it delivers chocolate with the cake while serving up some balanced panna cotta as well. Feel free to serve them separately if you're looking for a simpler treat—while a dynamite pair, they are also beautiful on their own.

SERVES 9

MACROS PER SERVING

Net carbs: 10 grams
Protein: 9 grams
Fat: 48 grams
Calories: 508

TEMPERED CHOCOLATE

1 cup (168 grams) Lily's milk chocolate chips

SMOKED-MILK PANNA COTTA

1 tablespoon unflavored gelatin
¼ cup (59 milliliters) cold whole milk
2 cups (473 milliliters) heavy cream
¼ cup (48 grams) allulose
1 teaspoon vanilla extract
¼ teaspoon salt

CHOCOLATE FROSTING

1 cup (227 grams) unsalted butter, softened
½ cup (121 grams) cream cheese
2 tablespoons whole milk
¼ cup (42 grams) Lily's milk chocolate chips
¼ cup (28 grams) cocoa powder
¼ teaspoon salt
1 cup (130 grams) Swerve confectioners' sugar

CHOCOLATE CAKE

1½ cups (144 grams) almond flour
⅓ cup (68 grams) Swerve granular sugar
¼ cup (28 grams) cocoa powder
2 tablespoons espresso powder
1 tablespoon baking powder
1 teaspoon salt
⅓ cup (79 milliliters) unsweetened almond milk
3 eggs

TO ASSEMBLE

9 slices chocolate cake
¾ cup (204 grams) chocolate frosting
9 (2-ounce [59-milliliter]) smoked-milk panna cottas
6 ounces (170 grams) tempered chocolate

TEMPERED CHOCOLATE

In a double boiler over medium heat, bring the chocolate up to 110°F (43°C). Remove from the heat and let cool to 90°F (32°C). Spread evenly over a sheet of acetate or parchment paper and allow to harden.

SMOKED-MILK PANNA COTTA

In a small bowl, add the gelatin to the cold milk and allow to bloom for 10 minutes. Add the mixture to a small saucepan with the remaining ingredients and bring to a simmer over medium-low heat. Simmer for 10 minutes and remove from the heat. Add to a smoker and let smoke for 30 minutes (if you don't have a smoker, add 2 drops of liquid smoke to the panna cotta mixture and proceed with the recipe). Transfer to nine 2-ounce (59-milliliter) panna cotta molds and let cool overnight in the fridge.

CHOCOLATE FROSTING

In a medium bowl with an electric mixer, beat the butter, cream cheese, and milk together. In a double boiler over medium-low heat, melt the chocolate. Add the chocolate, cocoa powder, and salt to the butter mixture, beat to combine, and slowly add in the sugar with the mixer running. Beat until fully incorporated, light, and fluffy. Set aside.

CHOCOLATE CAKE

Grease a 9″ x 9″ (23 x 23 cm) pan and preheat the oven to 350°F (177°C). In a large bowl, mix together the almond flour, sugar, cocoa powder, espresso powder, baking powder, and salt. In a medium bowl, combine the almond milk and eggs and whisk until blended, then add to the dry ingredients. Fold together (do not overmix). Add to the prepared pan and bake for 20 to 30 minutes until firm and cooked through. Let cool.

TO ASSEMBLE

Remove the cooled cake from the pan. Cut into 3″ x 3″ (8 x 8 cm) squares, frost each square on all sides, then top each slice with a panna cotta and garnish with the tempered chocolate.

SERVES 2

MACROS PER SERVING

Net carbs: 10 grams
Protein: 5 grams
Fat: 36 grams
Calories: 384

HUMBLE BERRY COBBLER

Being able to enjoy fresh berries is one of the saving graces that keeps me on track during this diet. This dish is no hassle and versatile. I love serving it piping hot out of the oven with a scoop of whipped cream on top so the cream cools the cobbler as it hits my mouth.

BERRY COBBLER

- ¼ cup (59 milliliters) brewed jasmine tea
- ¼ cup (40 grams) quartered strawberries
- ¼ cup (36 grams) blackberries
- 2 tablespoons blueberries
- 2 teaspoons fruit pectin powder
- 1 tablespoon Swerve granular sugar (optional)
- Squeeze of lemon juice (optional)
- ½ cup (48 grams) almond flour
- ¼ cup (57 grams) cold unsalted butter
- ¼ cup (36 grams) Swerve brown sugar
- 1 teaspoon salt
- ½ teaspoon cinnamon
- Pinch of freshly grated nutmeg
- 1 to 2 teaspoons cold water

WHIPPED CREAM

- 1 cup (237 milliliters) heavy cream
- ¼ cup (33 grams) Swerve confectioners' sugar

TO ASSEMBLE

- 2 berry cobblers
- 4 tablespoons whipped cream
- Mint leaves, for garnish

BERRY COBBLER

Preheat the oven to 350°F (177°C). In a small saucepan over medium heat, simmer the tea, berries, and pectin until thickened and bubbling, about 5 minutes. If the berries are underripe, add 1 tablespoon of Swerve granular sugar and a squeeze of lemon juice. In a food processor, blend the flour, butter, brown sugar, salt, cinnamon, and nutmeg. Pulse until small pebbles form and then add droplets of cold water until the dough barely starts to come together. Divide the berry mixture between 2 ramekins and then crumble the cobbler mixture on top. Bake for 25 minutes, or until the top is golden brown. Let cool until warm.

WHIPPED CREAM

In a large bowl with an electric mixer, whip the cream and confectioners' sugar until stiff peaks form.

TO ASSEMBLE

Pipe about 2 tablespoons of whipped cream onto each warm cobbler with a star piping tip. Garnish with mint.

COCONUT CAKE

I never knew I needed to learn how to make coconut cake until I started playing around with this recipe. This was my favorite dessert during my keto adventures, and I love the simplicity of the dish. In Hawaii, we have a plethora of locally grown coconuts to choose from.

SERVES 6

MACROS PER SERVING

Net carbs: 7 grams
Protein: 12 grams
Fat: 42 grams
Calories: 454

COCONUT CREAM CHEESE FROSTING

¼ cup (57 grams) unsalted butter, softened
¼ cup (60 grams) cream cheese, softened
3 tablespoons heavy cream
1 cup (130 grams) Swerve confectioners' sugar
2 tablespoons unsweetened shredded coconut
1 tablespoon coconut oil (optional)

COCONUT CAKE

8 eggs, separated
2 teaspoons cream of tartar
½ cup (109 grams) coconut oil
¼ cup (48 grams) Swerve granular sugar
2 tablespoons allulose
1 teaspoon vanilla extract
¼ cup (30 grams) coconut flour
¼ cup (24 grams) almond flour
¼ teaspoon salt

TO ASSEMBLE

6 slices coconut cake
1½ cups (396 grams) coconut cream cheese frosting
6 tablespoons unsweetened shredded coconut

COCONUT CREAM CHEESE FROSTING

In a large bowl with an electric mixer, beat the butter, cream cheese, and cream until smooth. With the beater running, gradually add the confectioners' sugar along with the shredded coconut. If desired, add coconut oil at the end for a softer texture.

COCONUT CAKE

Preheat the oven to 350°F (177°C) and grease a 9" x 9" (23 x 23 cm) pan with cooking spray. In a large bowl with an electric mixer, whip the egg whites with the cream of tartar until stiff peaks form. Set aside. In a small bowl, whisk together the egg yolks, coconut oil, granular sugar, allulose, and vanilla. Add the coconut flour, almond flour, and salt to the egg yolk mixture and blend. Fold in the whipped egg whites until no streaks remain. Pour into the prepared pan and bake for 20 minutes, or until golden brown. Cool and cut into 6 portions.

TO ASSEMBLE

Slice each portion in half horizontally to make 12 slices. Pipe half of the frosting onto 6 of the slices and spread evenly. Add the second layer of cake and pipe on the remaining frosting. Sprinkle the shredded coconut evenly over the top.

BERRY MOUSSE AND CURD TARTLET

Curd is the word. I didn't know what to expect while balancing all the acidity from the lemon with an artificial sugar, but the result was delicious and hit all the notes to cure my cravings. These components go great together or just served alongside a bowl of berries. Use whatever mold you like for the crust to make the tart into any portion size. I like to make smaller bite-sized tartlets to make portion control easy. Baking times will vary depending on the size you use.

SERVES 2

MACROS PER SERVING

Net carbs: 5 grams
Protein: 25 grams
Fat: 10 grams
Calories: 405

BERRY MOUSSE

2 egg whites
1 teaspoon cream of tartar
½ cup (118 milliliters) heavy cream
¼ cup (48 grams) Swerve granular sugar
2 teaspoons lemon zest
3 blackberries

SWEET PIE CRUST

1 cup (96 grams) almond flour
¼ cup (48 grams) Swerve granular sugar
¼ cup (57 grams) unsalted butter
1 egg
½ teaspoon baking soda
Pinch of salt
1 to 2 teaspoons ice water

LEMON CURD

¼ cup (59 milliliters) lemon juice
8 egg yolks
¼ cup (48 grams) Swerve granular sugar
¼ cup (48 grams) allulose
Pinch of salt

TO ASSEMBLE

6 tablespoons lemon curd
2 sweet pie crusts, cooked
8 blackberries
2 tablespoons Swerve confectioners' sugar
½ cup (85 grams) berry mousse

BERRY MOUSSE

In a large bowl with an electric mixer, beat the egg whites and cream of tartar together until stiff peaks form. In a separate medium bowl, also with the electric mixer, beat the remaining ingredients until stiff peaks form. Fold the mixtures together until no streaks remain. Pour into a piping bag and let set in the fridge for at least 2 hours. Once set, pipe ¼ cup (43 grams) into each of 2 serving cups and keep refrigerated until serving.

SWEET PIE CRUST

Grease 2 small metal tart pans—I use 3″ x 1″ (8 x 2.5 cm) oval pans. Preheat the oven to 350°F (177°C). Mix all the ingredients except the ice water until crumbly; add ice water as needed 1 teaspoon at a time until the dough just comes together. Wrap the dough in plastic wrap and put in the freezer for 20 minutes. On a surface lightly floured with almond flour, roll out the dough to about ¼″ (0.5 cm) thickness, then press into the prepared pans and prick all over with a fork. Bake for 15 minutes, or until golden brown. Let cool, then remove from the tart pans and set aside.

LEMON CURD

In a double boiler over medium-low heat, whisk the lemon juice, egg yolks, sugar, allulose, and salt together. Whisk constantly and remove from the heat every minute or so to make sure the eggs do not curdle. Whisk and cook until thick enough to coat the back of a spoon, 15 to 20 minutes. Remove from the heat, transfer to a pastry bag, and place in the fridge to cool.

TO ASSEMBLE

Pipe the curd evenly into the cooked crusts, layer on the blackberries, sift the confectioners' sugar on top, and serve with the cups of mousse on the side.

SIDE COMPONENTS

GUACAMOLE AND CHICHARRONES

SERVES 2

MACROS PER SERVING

Net carbs: 6 grams
Protein: 28 grams
Fat: 43 grams
Calories: 523

CILANTRO OIL

1 cup (237 milliliters) canola oil
2 bunches cilantro

TO ASSEMBLE

1 avocado
2 tablespoons minced shallots
2 teaspoons lime juice
1 teaspoon salt
4 blackberries, halved
2 tablespoons cotija cheese
2 to 3 kale chips
Microgreens, for garnish
3 tablespoons cilantro oil
1 cup (30 grams) chicharrones

CILANTRO OIL

In a high-powered blender, blend the oil and cilantro for 8 to 10 minutes. Let sit for 10 minutes and then strain through cheesecloth. Discard the solids.

TO ASSEMBLE

In a medium bowl, use a fork to mix the avocado, shallots, lime juice, and salt until a slightly chunky consistency is achieved. Add the blackberries and gently fold in. Add to a mold, turn onto a plate, and top with cotija, kale chips, and microgreens. Pour the cilantro oil around the guacamole. Serve with a side of chicharrones.

LAVENDER OLIVE MIX

SERVES 4

MACROS PER SERVING

Net carbs: 3 grams
Protein: 0 grams
Fat: 27 grams
Calories: 255

GREEN ONION CURLS

2 green onions

TO ASSEMBLE

1 quart (946 milliliters) olive oil
¼ cup (60 grams) kalamata olives
¼ cup (60 grams) Castelvetrano olives
¼ cup (70 grams) Cerignola olives
4 tablespoons lavender blossoms
½ bulb fennel, shaved
2 tablespoons green onion curls
1 tablespoon chili flakes
2 teaspoons salt
1 teaspoon fennel seed, toasted and ground
1 teaspoon coriander seed, toasted and ground
4 strips lemon peel
4 strips orange peel

GREEN ONION CURLS

Cut green onions thinly on the bias, then soak in ice water for at least 1 hour and up to 2 days.

TO ASSEMBLE

Add everything to a medium saucepan. Over medium-low heat, slowly bring to a simmer and cook for 5 minutes, then turn off the heat. Cool fully to room temperature before serving. Store in the fridge for up to 2 weeks.

SERVES 8

MACROS PER SERVING

Net carbs: 1 gram
Protein: 1 gram
Fat: 0 grams
Calories: 8

KIMCHI

Add the cabbage to a large bowl, toss in the salt, and let stand for 2 hours. Squeeze the cabbage to wring out excess moisture and discard the liquid. Add the remaining ingredients to the cabbage and mix until it is homogeneous. Place the contents in a sterilized container and top with a sterilized weight to press out any remaining air. Cover the top with cheesecloth and secure with butcher's twine, then let it ferment in a cool, dark place for 4 days undisturbed. Transfer to a new container and store in the fridge.

- 2 pounds (907 grams) green Napa cabbage, cut into large dice
- 2 tablespoons salt
- ½ cup (58 grams) Korean chili flakes (such as Wang brand)
- 4 tablespoons sea beans (optional)
- ½ bunch green onions, chopped into 2″ (5 cm) segments
- 3 tablespoons fish sauce
- 1 tablespoon sambal (such as Huy Fong sambal oelek)
- 2 teaspoons minced garlic
- 2 teaspoons unsweetened rice wine vinegar
- 2 teaspoons Swerve sugar
- Zest and juice from 1 lemon

SERVES 4

MACROS PER SERVING

Net carbs: 3 grams
Protein: 1 gram
Fat: 0 grams
Calories: 16

CORIANDER SAUERKRAUT

Chiffonade (finely slice) the cabbage, add to a large bowl, and mix in the salt, sugar, caraway, and garlic. Using your hands, squeeze and bruise the cabbage until juice forms. Place the cabbage mixture in a sterilized container and top with a sterilized weight, using the weight to press the mixture down until fully covered by its own juices. Cover the top of the container with cheesecloth and secure with butcher's twine. Allow to sit out in a cool, dark place for 2 to 3 weeks until souring flavor develops, checking every 2 to 3 days to ensure full submersion. When finished, toss lightly with the coriander and fennel fronds.

TIP: Fermenting food can result in dangerous and bad bacteria at times, so if a bad odor or lots of colored mold appears, don't hesitate to throw the batch away. If you're looking for a high-quality, store-bought version, look in the refrigerated section for lacto-fermented sauerkraut.

- 1 head green cabbage
- 2 tablespoons salt
- 1 tablespoon Swerve sugar
- 1 teaspoon caraway seed
- 2 cloves garlic, minced
- 2 teaspoons coriander seed, toasted and ground
- 3 sprigs fennel fronds

- 1 cup (341 grams) shredded green cabbage
- ¼ cup (43 grams) diced tricolor peppers
- 2 tablespoons sambal (such as Huy Fong sambal oelek)
- 1 teaspoon lemon juice
- 1 teaspoon lemon zest
- ½ teaspoon salt

SAMBAL SLAW

In a medium bowl, combine the ingredients and mix well. Let chill and serve.

SERVES 4

MACROS PER SERVING

Net carbs: 3 grams
Protein: 2 grams
Fat: 2 grams
Calories: 39

- 1 cup (59 grams) king trumpet mushrooms (ali'i)
- 1 cup (59 grams) beech mushrooms
- 1 cup (59 grams) maitake mushrooms
- 2 tablespoons olive oil
- 2 tablespoons unsalted butter
- 1 tablespoon minced garlic
- 1 tablespoon minced shallots
- 1 teaspoon fresh thyme
- 1 teaspoon lemon zest
- 1½ tablespoons XO sherry vinegar
- Salt and pepper

CARAMELIZED MUSHROOM MIX

Cut the mushrooms into quarters. Heat a large pan over high heat until very hot. Pour in the olive oil and add the mushrooms. Toss to coat with the oil, reduce to medium-high heat, and then sear the mushrooms without moving them for several minutes. Once the bottoms are golden brown, toss and cook on both sides. When the mushrooms are fully cooked, add the butter, garlic, shallots, thyme, and lemon zest. Toss for 30 seconds, add the vinegar to deglaze the pan, then remove from the heat. Season with salt and pepper and serve warm or at room temperature.

SERVES 4

MACROS PER SERVING

Net carbs: 10 grams
Protein: 6 grams
Fat: 54 grams
Calories: 137

SERVES 2

MACROS PER SERVING

Net carbs: 4 grams
Protein: 2 grams
Fat: 1 gram
Calories: 34

GARLICKY DILL PICKLES

Cool cucumbers with ice until quite cold. Remove ice, drain cucumbers, and add to a large jar or container. In a small bowl, mix the remaining ingredients, then pour over the cucumbers. Leave out at room temperature for 2 days, covered. Transfer container to the fridge to store.

- 1½ pounds (680 grams) pickling cucumbers
- 1 quart (946 milliliters) distilled white vinegar
- 1 quart (946 milliliters) water
- 2 tablespoons salt
- 1 tablespoon mustard seed
- 5 cloves garlic
- 4 sprigs dill
- 2 bay leaves
- 4 tablespoons capers, rinsed and drained

RESOURCES

GLOSSARY OF TECHNIQUES

Brunoise: This is the finest level of dicing before the food in question is considered minced. For a brunoise cut, first start with a julienne cut (see below), then dice into cubes of about ⅛ inch (3 mm).

Clarifying butter: To clarify butter, you remove water and milk solids and are left with pure butterfat, which has a much higher smoke point than regular butter. To make it, simply melt unsalted butter over low heat for about five minutes, or until some foamy solids have risen to the top. Skim the solids off, then carefully ladle the clear, golden butterfat into a separate container, leaving the remaining separated milk solids and water at the bottom of the pot.

Julienne: This classic cut involves turning a vegetable into evenly cut, matchstick-sized pieces. To do so, cut the vegetable lengthwise into planks about ⅛ inch (3 mm) thick. Then cut the planks lengthwise into ⅛ inch (3 mm-) thick sticks.

Quenelle: A traditional French technique of mixing creamy fish or meat into an egg-like shape and then poaching it. This elegant, oval-shaped scoop can also be applied to any soft, creamy substance (think ice cream or pâté). To make one, drag a spoon across the surface of the food in one direction, then swiftly turn the spoon and drag it back in the other direction to form a smooth oblong shape.

PRODUCT RECOMMENDATIONS

iSi: These devices whip liquid (like cream) using CO_2 or nitrous cartridges. They can create classic whipped cream or foams.

Sous vide immersion circulator: Sous vide cooking involves sealing food in an airtight plastic bag and cooking it in a water bath set to a constant temperature. An immersion circulator is inserted into water and heats it consistently while the food cooks to perfection. I recommend PolyScience.

Smoker: Indoor and outdoor smokers offer home cooks the opportunity to cook food at low temperatures with smoke, yielding delicious results. Traeger makes excellent smokers.

PARTNER PROFILES

FARMS

Working with farms will greatly increase the quality of food you make. This is just a basic rule of thumb for cooking. Go to the source, get it when it's in season, and most likely it will be superior in flavor, abundant, and favorable for your wallet. Frequent your local farmers' market and strike up a conversation with the farmers who grow that good *good*. Give them your money and keep going back. Local farms need support, and giving money directly helps ensure their survival.

For this cookbook I worked exclusively with Hua Momona Farms here on Maui. The farmers are Travis, Tina, and Zach, former hospitality workers who teamed up with the visionary owner, Gary Grube, who invested in this beautiful land for the past five years to grow sustainable organic produce. By applying its customer-driven mission and core values of uncompromising integrity and constant respect for people, the farm has become a leader in microgreens in Hawaii. I now live and work on the farm and harvest my own ingredients. Make cooking keto easy and delicious by supporting your local farm. If you don't know where to start, search online for "farmers' markets near me" and go from there.

TSAR NICOULAI

Caviar is a gift and a privilege to indulge in. The majority of Americans are not accustomed to fish roe, and the reasons are clear and understandable. Fish eggs can be intimidating for the shy eater by their very nature, not to mention expensive compared to other indulgences, pound for pound. Most have never tried salmon or trout roe. Tsar Nicoulai is your answer for affordable, impeccable caviar. You might notice there are a disproportionate number of dishes with caviar in this book. The main reason for this is that roe is an excellent source of omega fatty acids and protein. Caviar adds salinity, umami, and a sea breeze of

A's

freshness to fatty foods. I like to use caviar to balance flavors. It is distinct and heavenly.

I eat a lot of caviar compared to most people, and I use Tsar Nicoulai caviar exclusively. They are a US-based sustainable caviar company that produces high-quality roe on their farm in Wilton, California. Various types of their roes can be found in the market now at Whole Foods and Costco. I have worked in partnerships with Tsar Nicoulai over the years, and they have always generously given me samples for charity and experiments. I found that the majority of people who have never tried good caviar change their perspective quickly after trying a bump of some white sturgeon roe. I implore you to spoil yourself while you're on your keto journey and give it a try. Feel free to buy directly from their website at Tsarnicoulai.com and check out more of my caviar creations.

RAK PORCELAIN

We eat with our eyes first. When we are plating creative food, the serving vessel should be demonstrative of the quality of the cuisine. During the pandemic, we were lucky enough to be sponsored by Rak Porcelain to use their amazing plateware to play and create. Rak specializes in the crafting, manufacturing, and supplying of exquisite tableware. A huge thank you to the company and distributors who worked with us while the supply chain had terrible shortages.

THANKS

A huge thank you to everyone involved with the production of this book.

Lahaina Loft: Denise Black, who let us use her facility to host nonprofit fundraisers and feed over three thousand *kupuna* (elders) during the pandemic. The Chef Collective for Covid could not have functioned without your support. I am forever grateful for being given the opportunity to cook for the West Maui ohana.

Hua Momona Farms and Foundation: Gary Grube, who has given me the opportunity to use my culinary skills to help support the food security needs in Maui. After I lost everything in the fires, the foundation gave me a home, quite literally, and a purpose that gave me the ability to finish the book and prosper.

Tsar Nicoulai Caviar: Ali and Marai Bolourchi, and Otto Szilagyi, who have always supported whatever creative endeavors I chose to pour my passion into. They have never said no and have had a major impact on Bay Area and Maui philanthropy.

Bootjack Design: James van Kriedt, who gave his designing expertise and advice whenever I asked and has been a huge influence on my ethos and creative process.

Hans Bennewitz: The designer who stepped in to help tie up all the loose ends of the book and patiently worked with Keith and me to find available time to finally compile and endlessly edit the content we created.

Dennis King: Who graciously read through and edited my book. His guidance, perspective, and cheerleading have been an enormous force in finalizing this book.

A host of friends who helped donate time, effort, love, and assistance to give us the strength to finish this project: Michelle King, Heather Regan, Ryan Incerpi, and my brother Ross Raffin.

The Maui community, who have overwhelmed me with warmth and kindness from my first arrival. Hopefully this book will make them proud.

And a final big thank you to my partner in crime, Keith Schikore. Without his encouragement, friendship, and hard work, this book would have been impossible.

INDEX

C

D

E

F

G

H

I

T

W

X

Y

Z

ABOUT THE AUTHOR

JASON RAFFIN is a longtime chef and restaurateur. Having graduated from the Culinary Institute of America Greystone, Raffin worked in Napa Valley and San Francisco before co-opening the popular Scotland Yard. He went on to lead the culinary teams at Finn Town Tavern and Comstock Saloon before moving to Maui in 2020. There, he founded the nonprofit Chef Collective for Covid to fund local farms, empower regional chefs, and feed vulnerable communities. Meanwhile, he continued to work as the executive chef consultant for San Francisco restaurants such as Mission Street Burgers and Curio, as well as being the owner of Ali'i Chefs and Caterers. In the wake of the Maui fires of 2023, he became the executive chef of the Hua Momona Foundation in Lahaina. He lives and works on Maui.

ABOUT THE PHOTOGRAPHER

KEITH SCHIKORE studied biology at UC Santa Cruz, but instead of heading to optometry school, he returned to his roots in filmmaking and photography. In the San Francisco Bay Area, he managed day-to-day operations of the nonprofit Futures Explored for their Film & Media Workshop, which teaches filmmaking to people with developmental disabilities, emphasizing that all people have something valuable to contribute to the world. He also worked for ESPN and the local TV station covering the San Francisco Giants. He currently resides in Los Angeles and splits his time as a cinematographer and video editor—whenever not photographing and eating the delicious creations of Chef Jason.